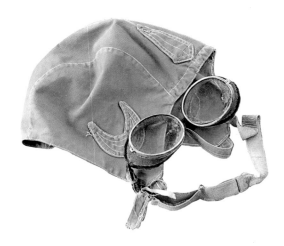

Juan Manuel
Fangio

Fangio, 'Negrita', and the Balcarce Autodrome, 1990.

FANGIO

A PIRELLI ALBUM

BY STIRLING MOSS

With Doug Nye

IN ASSOCIATION WITH

MERCEDES-BENZ

PAVILION

We first met Juan Manuel Fangio when he came to London to be guest of honour at the international press launch of our first book, *With Flying Colours: the Pirelli Album of Motor Sport*, in April 1987. From that moment, we resolved to publish our kind of book about this distinguished yet modest man, who so impressed us with his quiet dignity. To us, Juan Manuel Fangio is not only the greatest of all motor racing World Champions. He is also a very special human being, to whom we offer this tribute in affection and with unreserved admiration.

Robert Newman   Derek Forsyth.

First published in Great Britain in 1991 by
PAVILION BOOKS LIMITED
196 Shaftesbury Avenue,
London, WC2H 8JL

Fangio: A Pirelli Album Copyright © Pirelli Coordinamento Pneumatici SpA 1991

Text Copyright © Stirling Moss and Doug Nye 1991
Specially commissioned photographs Copyright © Phil Sayer 1991
Concept and co-producer Robert Newman
Art Director and co-producer Derek Forsyth
Designed by Derek Forsyth & Partners
Designer Erica Hare
Illustrations Peter Bowman

A CIP catalogue record for this book is available from the British Library

ISBN 1 85145 672 4

10 9 8 7 6 5 4 3 2 1

Printed and bound in Italy
by Amilcare Pizzi s.p.a.

The publication of Fangio: A Pirelli Album *represents the culmination of the recognition of one of our greatest sportsmen, who displayed his mastery on the track all over the world.*

It is also a most important tribute to this Argentine man who, through hard work, discipline and courage, brought national motor racing to the attention of the world.

I was but a boy when our beloved 'Chueco' was already a living legend; we all wanted to emulate him, to be just like him.

Thus, with Juan Manuel Fangio as an exceptional model, I grew up as did so many other Argentines, with a pride and passion difficult to describe, perhaps, because those curious privileges which life confers on us, years later, meant that I came to be included amongst the idol's friends.

Today, Juan Manuel Fangio no longer races on the tracks to carry off yet another victory, but he is still a winner, he is still present, because he has – quite simply – that quality of greatness.

And while this album represents universal recognition of a sporting career, it seems to me appropriate to recall that, for over 40 years, Fangio was an unofficial ambassador of Argentina, taking with pride and dignity, with his humble greatness, a positive image of our country all over the world.

Today, more than ever before, as our country enters a phase of positive achievement, the figure of Fangio acquires a central importance – as a human being and as a sportsman – for present and future generations.

So it is that, on behalf of the Argentine people and of myself, I send warmest greetings to this Argentine man who continues to fill us with pride.

Dr. Carlos S. Menem
President of the Republic of Argentina
APRIL 1991

Monaco Grand Prix, 1990.

JUAN MANUEL FANGIO, to many the greatest racing driver the world has ever known, was born in the country town of Balcarce, Argentina, on 24 June 1911. This Pirelli album has been published to commemorate the 80th anniversary of Fangio's birth and as a tribute to him as the winner of a record five Drivers' World Championship titles.

Mercedes-Benz

CONTENTS

Moss and Fangio, British Grand Prix,
Aintree, 1955 – Stirling won his
first GP, and Mercedes were 1-2-3-4.

The King and I

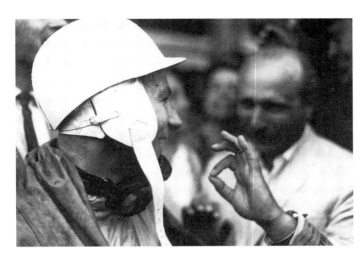

After Stirling's last GP win, Nürburgring, 1961.

I suppose the critical year was 1949. That was the season in which I drove in my first Continental races, and coincidentally it was also the first serious European season for Juan Fangio. To that extent our frontline careers took off around the same time, and over the next ten years they developed more or less in parallel. We eventually became team-mates – first with BRM, which I prefer to forget, and then at Mercedes-Benz, which I shall never forget. Through 1956 into 1958 we were rivals and we enjoyed some rare old battles as he became five-times World Champion Driver and I did my darndest to steal his crown.

That was an honourable period of motor racing, and regardless of whether we were team-mates or rivals I became fortunate enough to count Fangio as my friend, in many ways as a mentor, and always as the complete master of our sport.

Looking back now, it seems rather ignominious, but the first time I actually drove in the same race as Fangio I was forced to retire when – of all things – my chain broke. That was in July 1949. I was only 19 and Juan won't thank me for reminding him that at 38 he was then twice my age. The race in question was the charmingly-entitled Coupe des Petites Cylindrées at Reims in France, and while he started from pole position in a Ferrari and set fastest lap before his gearbox packed up, I started four rows behind him and it was the drive chain in my air-cooled rear-engined 'two-way' Cooper that let me down.

That 'two-way' Cooper could be fitted with either a single-cylinder JAP engine for 500cc racing, or a 1000cc twin-cylinder to take on the proper 2-litre cars in Formula 2. I was fresh from a race at Garda in Italy, where the Italian *tifosi* had first thought my quaint little car was hilarious – christening it 'The Jukebox' – and then made an enormous fuss of me because I managed to finish third in it amongst the Ferraris. Fangio, meanwhile, had of course been making bigger headlines. He had burst spectacularly upon the scene in his Maserati, sponsored by the Automobile Club of Argentina, and had won an entire string of Formula 1 races. Alfa Romeo were poised to sign him up for their 1950 Grand Prix team and his true class was about to be fully realised.

While he battled Farina for the inaugural World Championship title that year in the Alfa Romeos, I was invited to join the little British HWM Formula 2 team run by John Heath and George Abecassis.

John Heath had designed his 2-litre Alta-engined HWMs to be equally at home in long-distance sports car races or in Formula 2 – running in the former events with mudguards and lights fitted and in the latter with them removed. Pure-bred racing cars they were not! The driver's seat was offset to the right-hand side in a sober-looking stubby body. But they were nicely balanced little cars which enabled my regular team-mate Lance Macklin, myself and our occasional guest drivers in the third car, to drive them terribly hard right up to their limits, and most of the time well beyond.

Back at Reims that midsummer, we finished third, fourth and fifth, and then began a fantastic long-haul drive to Bari on the Italian coast where our form had won us entries into the local club's big Formula 1 race the following weekend.

The worn out HWM transporters had to cover a thousand miles in three days, and after all kinds of drama along the way one of our cars caught fire while being prepared in the garage we rented in Bari. It was badly scorched and blistered, but after yet another all-nighter those three little cars were pushed to the start-line before a huge crowd looking absolutely immaculate.

All eyes were on the opposition – Nino Farina and Fangio in the all-conquering factory *Alfettas*, a full Ferrari team and the two-stage supercharged Maseratis. My team-mates for HWM were Lance Macklin and the Swiss privateer, Rudi Fischer. Sitting there on the grid I knew the street and promenade circuit might suit the HWM and I was determined to make the Formula 1 boys work for their money.

As luck would have it, in the confusion after our garage fire, Lance's HWM had gone to the line with no oil in its back axle which promptly seized beneath him at around 130 mph, and Rudi Fischer retired with carburettor trouble. But my HWM ran like a bird and I had a lovely time, harrying the Formula 1 cars for all I was worth.

I eventually finished third behind Farina and Fangio's *Alfettas* but one incident during that race is imprinted vividly on my memory. I was actually ahead of them both at one stage, diving down into a corner when Farina came barging past under braking. He was never a man to trifle with drivers he saw as lesser mortals, and certainly no 20-year old kid – especially an English kid in a green car – was going to be shown any mercy by him!

So he barrelled past me into this particular turn, only to

Maserati drivers both, Belgian GP, Spa, 1954.

realise immediately that he had gone in too fast, and too deep, and his car was inevitably running out wide towards the straw bales on the exit. He was forced to back-off the throttle to save the situation, and as he did so I accelerated as hard as I could and my HWM scuttled up the inside and re-passed him.

Of course my glory was extremely brief as Farina quickly gathered himself together, selected a lower gear and blasted back past me, using all his extra 260-odd horsepower. And right on his heels came Fangio, who had been sitting close behind watching the whole thing develop before him. As he boomed by I glanced across at him, and where Farina's face had been set in a dark and angry scowl, Fangio looked at me and I saw he was laughing like a drain! He'd enjoyed the whole episode immensely.

That was a thrilling, warming moment. Right then, my heart went out to the stocky, modest man from Argentina – and I never discovered anything subsequently to make me modify this first reaction.

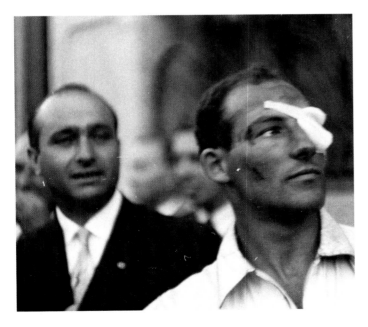

Dangers of 'The Train' – after following the Maestro too closely in the Mercedes, Dutch GP, 1955.

Stirling Moss 1991

Four-year old Juan Fangio, elder brother José and sisters Celia and Herminia.

Mama and Papa – dona Herminia and don Loretto Fangio.

The Boy from Balcarce – First Communion, 11 years old.

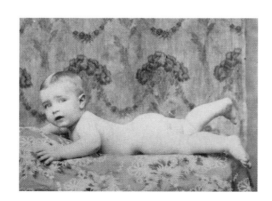

Juan five months old.

1911-1931: The Boy from Balcarce

Sit down with Juan Fangio today to discuss his glittering career and one of the first questions you might ask is 'Which period of your career do you regard as having been the most important?' The answer might surprise you. It's not the years of those unmatched five World Championship titles. Oh no. Instead, he'll say flatly 'My early career, the South American part. That's the beginning of the story and it's the beginnings that are important in life. It's a young man's early life, and the struggling years of a career, that form his character and make him into the man he will be for ever more.'

This kind of simple, logical philosophizing is as typically Fangio as his impeccable good manners, his constant thought for others, and his abiding unhurried calm. He always has time for everybody, and anybody.

He'll tell you: 'My childhood was very happy. My parents were by no means rich, but of course by comparison with most children today we expected very little from life; so whatever was provided for us we saw as a bonus.'

Even today, Balcarce in Buenos Aires province, Argentina, is a humble agricultural town. It's a centre of what in England we call market gardening, the area producing vegetables – especially potatoes – for the capital, 400kms to the north.

Juan's father, *don* Loreto Fangio, was an immigrant Italian, his mother a first-generation Argentine of Italian stock. Both sets of grandparents had originated from Chieti, in the Italian Abruzzi, where they had grown up in villages barely 50kms apart, the Fangios in Castiglione Messer Marino and the Deramos in Tornarece.

Grandfather Giuseppe Fangio had arrived in Argentina in 1887. He worked charcoal until he'd saved sufficient money to buy a 10-hectare farm just outside Balcarce, and

summoned his family – including Loreto, Juan's father, then aged seven – to join him from Italy. Loreto married Herminia on 24 October 1903 when he was 19, and she only 17.

After first earning his living on the land, *don* Loreto became a stonemason's labourer. From his wages he began to buy by instalments a plot of land in Balcarce, where he built himself a home. He brought *dona* Herminia there, and they started their family. As the kids were born, *don* Loreto extended his house to accommodate them. There were six children; José, Herminia, Celia, then Juan, Carmen and Ruben.

Juan was born in 1911, on 24 June – the Day of St John – while *don* Loreto – an ardent Royalist – chose his second name 'Manuel' in honour of the Italian King. Years later, *don* Loreto sold some of his plot on what had been renamed 13th Street, Balcarce, to his father-in-law – who was a builder – and who also erected a house there. And as Juan explains to visitors today 'Papa also sold land to my uncles as well, which went on to their children and so today nearly all our neighbours here are relatives. For me the support of family, and especially of my friends in Balcarce, has always been the most important thing. They helped me immensely from the very beginning, and without them I would never have had the chance to begin my racing.

'At school, I was good at maths. All young boys then were expected to learn a trade, but I didn't want to be a stonemason like my father. Instead, Papa got me a place with Francisco Cerri, the blacksmith.'

Juan had already been introduced to the motor car. 'a single-cylinder owned by a neighbour, a Senor Carta. I was fascinated by the thing.

'My father was anxious I should have the best

education he could provide. This involved me getting up at 4 am every morning to study, then going to school in the morning, then to the smithy in the afternoon. My apprenticeship continued – working seven days a week – in a workshop owned by Capettini. It was there that I drove a car for the first time.

'I cleaned everything, cleaned parts, always cleaning but learning all the time. I watched how Capettini did things, and when he moved away I joined the Carlini brothers, the local agents for Rugby cars. They raced a Rugby with a special aluminium body.'

Juan moved on to the Estevez Ford agency's workshop, under a chief mechanic named Guillermo Spain, who took Juan along as his driver on call-outs to fix farm machinery.

At only 12, Juan became a junior mechanic at Miguel Viggiano's Studebaker agency, and after a couple of years was senior fitter there. He loved that mechanical work. 'At Viggiano's I could do what I liked, and what really fascinated me was that we had racing cars to work on in his shop.' Viggiano himself raced occasionally, and Manuel Ayerza, the pre-war Argentine road racing champion, had a Studebaker prepared there.

'It was hard work, you learned to improvise. Machine tools were virtually unknown. We had hammers and drills, spanners and screwdrivers. We also had emery stones and muscle and brain-power, and a succession of jobs which had to be done with the tools available. So we did it. The racers, Viggiano and Ayerza, used to hand-file their special camshafts to shape. We used to salvage damaged cylinder heads by stoning them smooth, just scrubbing away at them, hour after hour.'

Viggiano trusted Juan to deliver and collect custom-ers' cars. But tarmac roads were rare at that time. The normal surface away from the big cities was packed dirt, and whenever it rained hard the roads between Balcarce and Buenos Aires could become impassably boggy. Juan recalls: 'Viggiano taught me a lot about driving. He showed me how to negotiate mud, to have a sensitive throttle foot, to minimize wheelspin, which would only dig you deeper into trouble. You shouldn't touch the brakes on slippery mud, always use the gearbox to slow down, to keep the car balanced, the wheels evenly loaded – I learned a lot of valuable driving lessons at a very receptive age.'

He left Balcarce's School No. 1 after the Sixth Grade, aged 12 to work for Viggiano. 'Eventually he owed me for a year's work! And he gave me an Indian motor-cycle instead. We went to try it out, he crashed and smashed its gearbox beyond repair. But he gave me instead an Overland four-cylinder car which I modified a bit and then thought – ha – this I could race. We took the body off and fitted a racing body in its place. I was 15 years old then. It was an illusion that it was a racing car. But I liked the illusion!'

Juan was a skilful footballer with the local 'Leandro N. Alem' club. 'I played inside-right. Because of my bow legs they called me *El Chueco*, but I was really quick, hardly any left-back could catch me.'

But he developed pleurisy and was nursed back to health by his mother, who feared he'd die. I had similar problems, developing nephritis when I was 11 or 12. Juan's pleurisy left its mark for a while – severe chest pain accompanying any extended effort, both in the workshop and on the soccer field. But at 20 he passed his military medical with flying colours and served a year with the 6th Artillery in the Campo de Mayo, Buenos Aires. The boy had become a man.

'El Chueco' – the demon inside-right
– Balcarce soccer team, 1933.

*Fangio – standing third right –
toughened-up a lot by Army service,
and yet more football.*

1932-1939: Novice Racer

By the time he entered the Army, Fangio had already had his first taste of racing, as 18 year-old passenger to none other than Manuel Ayerza in a 1928 four-cylinder Chevrolet. They ran from Coronel Vidal to Maipu on a dirt road, later surfaced as Argentina's Route 2. In the following year Juan's brother-in-law Brujas Font drove a '28, Plymouth on the La Chata circuit outside Balcarce with Juan again as riding mechanic.

He completed his military service at 21, in 1932, and a footballing future beckoned as he and his friend and team-mate José Duffard were offered places with a club in Mar del Plata.

'But our team-mates in Balcarce didn't want us to leave. Both José and I fixed cars, so they talked us into opening our own workshop in Balcarce, largely to keep us in their team. We started our business in a shed we built ourselves on part of Papa's land. Francisco Cavallotti – another of our team – was an accountant who worked for Carlini's Rugby agency, and he joined us and sensibly made us move to the town centre where eventually we took over an entire corner site.'

They named the company 'Fangio, Duffard y Cia'. Subsequently, Bernardo Duffard, José's older brother, and Juan's younger brother Ruben (Toto) also joined the firm.

'We built a reputation for doing good and careful work, inexpensively – in fact we had not learned to charge enough! But all the time I loved the idea of motor racing, which I thought would be good publicity for our firm.'

He made his driving début in an unsanctioned race, on Saturday 24 October 1936. The venue was the Benito Juárez track, and he drove a modified taxi.

'It was a 1929 Ford Model A, owned by the father of a friend of mine – "Pichon" Viangulli. We had removed its body and fitted instead an open two-seat shell. It was running on four brand new tyres bought for me by one of my customers, the Balcarce town councillor Oscar Raul Rezusta, who had council vehicles serviced by us. We were even loaned a spare wheel by another taxi-operator, Vigiano.

'I was ecstatic when I actually went out to race for the first time as a driver. Forget the prize money, I just dreamed of the good publicity for our company, of the custom it would bring us. My only worry was how to afford to prepare a car for racing. Without friends' help I could not race, because I had no money. Nor did I have a car unless I could borrow one.'

To hide his identity, Juan ran under the pseudonym 'Rivadavia' – as his Balcarce soccer club had been renamed. But *don* Loreto found out. Juan admits, 'Later Papa told me off, not for racing, but for letting him find out from somebody else.'

There was a thousand *pesos* prize at Benito Juárez but Juan's engine ran a big-end bearing when lying third. Having failed to earn one *centavo*, he now had to restore Viangulli's taxi to the order in which it had been provided.

'But another friend, Leonardo Yalea's father, then loaned me his 1930 Model A Ford which had already been prepared for racing and within two months I was out on the track again.'

The venue this time was González Chávez: 'We were delayed leaving for the circuit on the Sunday morning and arrived after the race had started. I just joined in a lap behind, but ahead of the leader on the road so people thought I was winning, until I was disqualified. It was stupid; we returned to Balcarce very depressed.'

After that rebuff, Juan concentrated upon the garage

Fangio and brother Toto in their garage, Balcarce 1990.

Fangio had his maiden 'outlaw' race in a borrowed Model A Ford special. This is the car he prepared for his friend Leonardo Yalea to drive at González Chávez in December, 1936.

*Fangio and Bianchilli on the line for
his first officially sanctioned race at
Necochea, 1938, in the
1934-chassised Ford V8 special.*

Ford V8, Balcarce 1990.

Juan ran the Ford V8 in three events through 1938-39, at Necochea, on the track at Tres Arroyos and at La Plata.

business into the new year – 1937 – until councillor Rezusta lent him an eight-cylinder Buick for another event at the local La Chata track. 'But as I selected first I jammed the gearbox. We fixed it, but then I hit a bridge. That meant more work for us to put it right. Racing was costing us a fortune in work we couldn't charge for.'

Friends kept the faith that Fangio could make it. They knew just how well he could drive on the road, and had confidence he could shine in competition.

Brother Toto urged him to buy a '34 Ford special with a current engine which had just won at La Chata; driven by José Cordonnier. Money was the problem, and again friends came to the rescue; 'Estebán and Juan Ezcurdia lent us 2000 *pesos* and we bought it.'

On 27 March 1938 an inaugural race was being held at Necochea offering a prize fund of 20,000 *pesos*. It was Fangio's first official race as a driver, and he finished fifth amongst 24 starters in the qualifying Heat, facing many infinitely more sophisticated cars. He was third in the official Heat and then seventh in the Final.

He also had his first experience of a major Carretera Turismo open-road race that year, sharing a '37 Ford two-door sedan with Luis Finochietti from Balcarce in the Argentine Motor Sport Committee's Gran Premio Argentino de Carreteras, run between 18 and 30 October.

THE ARGENTINE WAY OF RACING

In Europe at that time we had two mainstream branches of motor sport – circuit racing and rallying. Circuit racing extended from as little as three laps at Brooklands to as much as 24-Hours at Le Mans or Spa, and of course the pinnacle of circuit racing was pure-bred Grand Prix competition with single-seater open-wheeled racing cars. Rallying involved mainly sports-type cars, competing in events like the International Alpine Trial which extended over several days, with target average speeds to be achieved over difficult roads.

In Argentina, the split was between closed-track racing, and the Turismo Carretera kind of open-road racing, city-to-city. Here there was no question of achieving a target average speed. This was full-blooded racing, as in the Italian Mille Miglia: drivers were expected to pedal their touring cars along just as fast as their wheels could carry them, point-to-point on everyday (which meant largely unsurfaced) country roads.

These events were run often over immense distances, to last several days, with a number of individual Stages separated by occasional overnight stops or short neutralized-time sections through the main town centres. As in European rallying, the cars were impounded between Stages in Parcs Fermés, where repair work upon them was forbidden. They were then released from the Parcs perhaps one hour or half an hour before the next Stage started, allowing the crews that much time for necessary servicing.

The closed circuit Argentine track scene was open to all kinds of racing cars from European Grand Prix and American Indianapolis-type open-wheelers through modified sports cars to home-built specials. The tracks were dirt-surfaced and the racing was fast, hectic and dangerous.

Gran Premio Argentino, 1938 – Luis Finochietti and Fangio with the Ford Coupe, 7th after 7,389.8kms rough-road racing!

CARACAS

Mérida

VENEZUELA

BOGOTÁ

COLOMBIA

Popayán

QUITO

Tumbes

PERU

○ *ACCIDENT 1948*

LIMA   Avecucho

Cusco

BRAZIL

Gioânia

LA PAZ

Oruro

Potosi

Barretos   BELO HORIZONTE

La Quiaca

Petrópolis

Salta

S. PAULO   RIO DE JANEIRO
(Interlagos)   (Gavea and Boa Vista)

S. Miguel de Tucumán

ARGENTINA

Córdoba

Va. Maria
La Carlota   BUENOS AIRES

SANTIAGO   MONTEVIDEO

General Pico

Balcarce

Bahia Blanca

Trelew

Comodoro Rivadavia

Puerto Deseado

Rio Gallegos

PACIFIC OCEAN

CHILE

ATLANTIC OCEAN

———— G.P. INT. DEL NORTE, 1940

———— G.P. GETULIO VARGAS, 1941

———— G.P. DEL SUR, 1942

———— G.P. DE LA AMERICA

DEL SUR, 1948

*The sheer scale of South American
Carretera Turismo racing boggles the
mind of European enthusiasts and
makes Italy's classic Mille Miglia
look merely a sprint in comparison.*

*Nothing about Carretera racing was
easy – through these conditions Juan
finished 5th in the GP
· Extraordinario of 1939.*

Fangio and Hector Tieri with the Balcarce Chevrolet Coupe during the Gran Premio Argentino, 1939.

The 1938 Gran Premio de Carreteras involved Fangio and Finochietti in 4,590 miles of racing, in ten Stages, and they finished seventh. All Balcarce sat up and took notice. Then on 13 November 1938, Fangio tried his hand again at circuit racing, in the 400kms at Tres Arroyos, but five died, and the race was abandoned.

His '38-engined '34 Ford V8 had given him his introduction to legitimate racing. He ran it one last time, in May 1939, on the El Bosque circuit at Buenos Aires, finishing fifth in the qualifying Heat and then eighth in the Final. His passenger was a Ford mechanic named Hector Tieri who had just joined the Balcarce garage.

'My townsmen wanted me to do better, and they organized a collection to buy me a car for the Gran Premio that October.' Juan tried to buy a new '39 Ford. None was available, but the Alonso Chevrolet agency had a black '39 coupé on show which he bought instead.

In fact, as the Gran Premio set off on 19 October 1939, the Fangio/Tieri Chevvy was barely out of Buenos Aires before a big-end bearing ran and the oil pressure zeroed. They dropped the sump, replaced the bearing and rattled on, finishing the Stage in Santa Fe 108th overall.

For Stage 2, torrential rain had ruined the clay roads of Entre Rios province. Juan had rigged a rubber tube through a hole in the dashboard, so Tieri could feed extra oil from the cans they had with them down into the sump without stopping the car. But the damaged engine burned so much oil that a hot, stinking haze was blown back up the tube into the cabin.

Tieri had to blow it back into the sump and became

coated in black, sticky grime. Meanwhile the rain still pelted down and Juan was fighting the mud with all his specialized skills. The Chevrolet repeatedly bogged down.

'In one town, waving to spectators who had been waving to us, I got stuck. We both jumped out to help some soldiers push the car clear, but the mud was so deep it sucked off my shoes and I lost them. I drove on, barefoot.'

He had left Paraná 108th and arrived in Concordia 18th overall, ninth on time for the Stage. But the rain continued unabated, and the race was stopped right there. Its organisers immediately announced a Gran Premio Extraordinario to start a week later from Córdoba, avoiding the muddiest roads to Santiago del Estero, then along the route as originally planned. The cars were taken by rail to Córdoba, where Fangio rushed his straight to the GM agency for repair.

But race officials intervened to ensure he worked only with the parts and tools carried on the car itself. 'Then the GM rep insisted I should have a new crankshaft because mine was irreparably scored – it would be bad publicity for Chevrolet to continue with it like that. But he also insisted I should buy the replacement so I stormed out to find a better place to do my work. A taxi driver directed me to Ramaciotti's where workshop facilities were put at my disposal; and when I returned to the GM garage they did the same.

'A good workman named Stabio was the Fiat representative and he made a half bearing of brass to enclose the existing rear crankshaft bearing. There was a gap left which we fitted with a kind of gasket cut from the brim of a felt hat to act as an oil seal. This worked so well some other Chevrolet runners later copied the idea. I refitted the engine at the GM garage and then took the car to Ramaciotti's for final preparation.'

The GP Extraordinario began, and Juan finished eighth on the Santiago del Estero Stage, his car the leading Chevrolet. Of course radio was the most important means of mass communication in pre-war Argentina, and Manuel Sojit was already famous as a motor racing commentator, using the pseudonym 'Corner'. Juan introduced himself and was interviewed on air. Ten years later millions of Argentine homes would tune in to them talking motor racing, but from the other side of the World.

'On the next stage, Santiago-Jujuy, I was third, with only two Fords still in front, and the GM rep was there offering anything I wanted. I was so surprised I just asked for two new rear tyres, I didn't even have the sense to ask for a complete set of four!'

In the Balcarce car he was leading the Gran Premio overall until, approaching Mendoza, he threw it away. 'We were driving into the town in bright sunlight along a poplar-lined road, and the flickering sun and the brilliant contrast between light and shade through the dirty windscreen dazzled me. At a place called Palmira there was a tricky ess-bend which I simply didn't see. We left the road, broke the rear spring mounts, bent a wheel, busted the body mounts and wrenched the propshaft.'

They managed to press on but the car had no brakes and near Valde a half-shaft broke and the wheel came off. They ran the final 18 miles into San Luis with Juan's dreams of winning dashed. 'We were 44th out of 47 left.'

The Balcarce coupé was classified fifth overall — winning 2,000 *pesos*. That December saw Juan race the Chevrolet again, in the Mil Millas Argentinas, finishing 13th after further troubles. Maybe motor racing was not so easy after all?

Chevrolet and Fangio, Balcarce 1990.

1940-1942: *Champion of Argentina*

For 1940, the Competitions Committee of the ACA organised its most ambitious Carretera event yet, the Gran Premio Internacional del Norte. The route ran from Buenos Aires, northwards through Bolivia, to Lima in Peru, a distance of 2,962 miles during which the route soared above 13,000 feet. After two days' rest the surviving crews would then return to Buenos Aires, the total distance being 5,868 miles.

To limit the number of days this new 'Grand Prix of the North' would last, the ACA planners lengthened each individual stage – starting with Buenos Aires to Tucumán, 847 miles in one hit!*

Juan had to sell the '39 coupé (for 2,850 *pesos*) to settle his debts. Now he was desperate for another car to race. But times were hard. Nobody in Balcarce could help. Then his friends suggested Francisco Polio, the potato buyer from Mar del Plata. He used the Balcarce garage, and favoured Chevrolets.

Chevrolets were big in the potato business.

Juan asked for a little help in buying back the '39 coupé for the Gran Premio, but Polio, who bought his cars from the Navarro Brothers' agency in Mar del Plata believed the 1940 model had more power. Juan protested he could afford nothing so new.

Back in Balcarce his friends had decided that a raffle would generate the funds from ticket sales to buy Juan the car required. The car would be the prize – in whatever condition it might finish the race.

Since there was no prize car to see, ticket sales were slow. Polio then sent Juan to the Navarro agency to buy

Until that time, the longest open-road race Stage yet run had been 733 miles from Buenos Aires to Mendoza in 1935, in an event won by the good Uruguayan driver, Hector Suppici Sedes.

1940 GP Internacional del Norte – Tieri and Fangio – outright winners.

one, personally guaranteeing its cost. But there were no Chevvys in stock. At the last moment, another mutual friend, Juan di Pace, offered his own new low-mileage coupé. Polio promised di Pace a replacement as soon as one became available, so Fangio had his ride.

With the coupé on display, the thousand 10-*peso* tickets sold rapidly. While the raffle raised 10,000 *pesos* the car had cost Polio 3,500 and the Navarros threw in a spare wheel free!

On Friday 27 September 1940, the great race began from Buenos Aires' River Plate Stadium. At Córdoba Fangio's dark-green Chevrolet lay third. He needed to refuel in Concepción but the town square was so packed he pressed on and just made it, winning the long Stage at an average of 78mph. 'Tucumán even today holds happy memories for me.'

Oscar Gálvez then won Stages 2 and 3. Each one lasted six to eight hours, but at the stops the crews had to service the cars, fit fresh tyres, keep them going. Only then could they snatch some rest and food. 'We kept ourselves going by eating cloves of garlic and chewing coca leaves.'

The Stage ending in La Paz left only 10 minutes to get from the arrival checkpoint to the organisers' enclosure where President Enrique Peñaranda was presenting the laurels. 'I ran from the control, received the laurels, and ran back in time to see Tieri driving our car off down the slope, as someone had told him time was running out and we would be last into the Parc Fermé. But Bolivians drove on the right, not the left as in Argentina at that time,* and Tieri hit another car head-on.

'The impact bent the front axle and the ends of the chassis frame. We straightened it out as best we could and set off with the front wheels bouncing and wobbling and me cursing Tieri. We repaired it a little better at the end of the next Stage, and then the fan threw a blade which gashed the radiator.

The 1940 Chevrolet in the great race to the north.

* *Argentina changed over to driving on the right on 10 June 1945.*

We came into a village calling for water and the locals brought us glasses of water to drink! When we explained, they thought it was a huge joke. We topped-up, but it soon emptied again. Then we found a deserted roadworks depot with a water tank and like that we brought the car into Nazca on the last drop. We removed the radiator before entering the Parc Fermé, and spent much of that night repairing it with lead, using a candle and bellows.

'Next morning we refitted the radiator and topped up with water. We'd done everything but fit fresh tyres and we found ourselves too late to get any. We were tenth into Lima with the tyres through to the canvas, but we still led overall. This time I wasn't going to throw it away.'

Fangio tore back south towards Buenos Aires, but on Stage 9 he slid wide on a corner, struck a rock with the right-rear wheel and bent it and the halfshaft.

Pouring cooling water and daubing grease on the damaged prop shaft through a hole in the floor, Fangio and Tieri smoked on through Humahuaca, doubtful even of reaching Jujuy. Julio Perez caught them and shouted across. Fangio told him to press on and arrange for a diff to be ready to be fitted at the Jujuy Chevrolet dealers during the 30-minute scheduled break. Three GM mechanics and Juan himself changed the diff, just in time.

At Tucumán they received another heroes' welcome, and reaching Rosario at dawn 'the crowd was shouting my name. I wished Papa could have been there to hear it.'

Fangio won the great race from 31 other survivors, winning over 45,000 *pesos* in prize money and trade bonuses.

He paid the Navarro Brothers for the coupé. It was their mechanics who had bought the winning raffle ticket and Juan subsequently bought the car back from them for the 3,500 *pesos* it had originally cost, and agreed to paint 'Mar del Plata' on it for one race.

There was some friction at that time between Fangio and Hector Tieri. They ran together again in the Mil Millas Argentinas, and argued over how to fix the carburettor problems which dogged them. They finished eighth, and Tieri passengered Fangio no more. But that placing gave Juan his first major title, Argentine Carretera Champion of 1940.

Almost the entire population of Balcarce welcomed him home in triumph. He had taken his name and that of his town across frontiers to fame, and after 1940 Balcarce was more than just a potato town. It was home to the new Argentine Champion.

In the following year, despite the World War raging elsewhere, Juan defended his national title in neutral South America with wins in the Gran Premio Presidente Getulio

Dirt-tracking on the public roads 1941 Mil Millas Argentinos.

Vargas in Brazil in June, and the Argentine Mil Millas in December. For the Brazilian race he took a new companion, Antonio Elizalde. He was a Basque, not a mechanic but a humble car washer. 'And a good lad. I knew enough mechanically not to need a mechanic. Everyone told me I was just taking "a sack of potatoes" with me. But Elizalde was special. He was extremely conscientious – we never left anything behind when he was with me – and he had a fantastic memory – he could ride along a road once and remember every feature of it. He was great for warning me a dangerous corner was approaching if I showed signs of having forgotten it.'

For the Brazilian race, *don* Francisco Polio had just swopped his 1940 Chevrolet coupé for a '41 and he apparently lent the new car to Juan for the race, to be returned later. Juan fitted the car with an engine from a lorry, belonging to José Polio, brother of Francisco.

'We had to reconnoitre the course in the cars we would be racing. Almost 2,500 miles! That used up what little money we had brought with us. Chevrolet offered nothing, saying a Ford is sure to win. Just to get fresh tyres I had to pledge the car right before the start.'

The race covered 2,423 miles in seven Stages, of which Fangio and Oscar Gálvez promptly won six, the Brazilian Julio Veira the other by default. Gálvez had led Fangio the wrong way at a fork. 'We were the first into São Paulo but the news came we had not passed through Itapecerica, saving ourselves 40 miles. They were going to disqualify us but then said we should go back down the route and return by the right road. That was how Veira won the Stage, but then Oscar set record time to Rio on the final day.'

Juan won overall, earning enough to redeem his car

and ship it back home on the SS *Brazil*.

The Mil Millas followed, run over two Stages on 13 December. Fangio won, clinching the Carretera Championship for the second successive year.

Around that time, the ACA was talking of a new major race. The Gran Premio del Norte had been an epic event heading to the north, now the Gran Premio del Sur would extend competition far to the south.

Despite the threat of petrol rationing, the Gran Premio del Sur finally set off on 21 January 1942, from Mercedes, Buenos Aires province. Fangio finished tenth. 'But I was as happy as if I had won. It was the first time we'd been to Patagonia. I had known nothing of the terrain and climate. It was Indian country to me, so I drove the whole route in advance. In Chilean territory there was a stretch where the mud became so heavy in rain it was called "the chocolate". We covered the underside of our car with sacking to prevent stones breaking pipes or damaging the chassis. We knew it was going to be really tough.'

Stage 1 was dominated by Alfredo Pián, a driver making his road racing debut, who led to General Villegas at 83mph! But he did not finish the Stage which Gálvez won from Iraizos – a friend of Fangio's – and Juan himself.

On Stage 4, littered with large, loose stones, the Chevrolet's spring shackles were broken. Another stone smashed the windscreen. Elizalde removed his socks to tie into place what remained of the glass. They had no goggles, a storm broke over the course – 'It was like racing through a car-wash.' They did their best to fix each problem as it arose. Next day, Stage 7, soon after the restart near Comandante Luis Piedrabuena, the sump plug dropped out and the engine oil gushed away. Before Juan could catch it, a big-end seized and the engine broke a con-rod, smashing

His countrymen's encouragement meant the world to Juan. Here he storms into Bahia Blanca in the 1942 Gran Premio del Sur, and makes it to the finish in the much-repaired Chevrolet. Its wings were cut high to prevent mud and rocks accumulating inside and binding on the tyres.

a hole through the block.

'I dismantled the holed block, and we bought an aluminium cooking pot at a local store, which we used to make a patch. I fitted a rod, piston and rings from the spares we always carried and we reached the Stage finish at Puerto Deseado just before it closed. So we began the following Stage in 12th place – but only 14 were left in the race.'

He still inherited the lead on that Stage when Fernandino's gearbox broke in Rio Gallegos – 'But he'd pulled into a garage and we didn't see him as we went by. Consequently I thought I was still chasing him, so I forced on too hard and another con-rod broke and punched another hole in the block. It was impossible to repair beside the road, so when someone passed I asked them to send help. A lorry appeared, and we used it to tow the Chevrolet to Comandante Piedra Nueva with me driving and Elizalde steering the Chevrolet – on a short tow. We took it to a garage owned by a Chilean called Cardenas whom I'd got to know during my reconnaissance. He was a fine Chevrolet mechanic. We towed nearly 60 miles but still were not disqualified. The organizers were afraid no cars would finish!'

Juan won the last Stage to Bahia Blanca, and he and Elizalde were placed 10th overall. Their car used the '42 Chevrolet engine from a car just acquired new by *don* Francisco Polio's brother, José. Fangio had been worrying how he would react to the aluminium cooking pot repair to his block, but José Polio insisted on having the engine back as an honourable trophy. Juan really did have some wonderful friends.

Despite deepening austerity, the ACA managed to run their Gran Premio Circuito Mar y Sierras – a lovely name, meaning the 'Circuit of the Sea and Mountains' – three months after the Gran Premio del Sur, at Easter 1942.

This race started from the seaside at Mar del Plata and passed through Balcarce. Fangio was keen to put up a good show, but when the Chevrolet was checked over at the Navarros' agency its transmission was found to be badly worn. The foreman there, 'Lela' Lillo, had no spares, so they cannibalized the diff from Polio's '42 car but found it wouldn't fit, it was too big. 'We then persuaded one of the Navarros to loan us the part from his own '41 car – and when he was dubious, Polio assured him "If it breaks I'll pay for it." That was the kind of support they gave me.

'We started early in the morning, before dawn. It was dark and foggy and while the leaders had a clear road, I was eating their dust. I would close on the tail-lights of a car ahead, then pull out and catapult past it, using its headlights, but virtually blind. Near Villa Gesell I pulled out to pass like that and found myself heading straight – end-on – for a bridge parapet! I got through by chance and I won that race too.'

Again his mechanical ingenuity paid off. Across the marshland near Energïa the Chevrolet broke a spring. During the half-hour of neutral time at Necochea, Fangio and three helpers tore off the Chevrolet's heavy-gauge steel rear bumper and fashioned two new spring leaves from it, to replace the broken ones. Juan won after the leader, Alcuaz, had broken his gearbox.

That was the end of pre-war road racing in Argentina. Track racing, in which Fangio played no part at that time, continued through two more events. Then four years of darkness descended for Argentine motor racing.

1942-1947: Wartime and Beyond

When motor racing in Argentina was suspended due to the wartime shortages and restrictions of 1942-45, Fangio was already 31 years old. As an enthusiastic racing driver he worried that by the time the sport resumed he might be past his best – too old. But as an astute motor trader he looked around for a viable means of income. There was no shortage of food, but any manufactured goods were scarce. So was oil, and particularly rubber. Fuel was rationed but was at least available, unlike new tyres. People from Buenos Aires would drive out into the rural areas like Balcarce looking to buy worn but usable tyres at almost any price.

As economic activity suffocated, some hauliers sold their trucks. Others simply ran out of fuel coupons and, since it was illegal to buy more, they sold the trucks they could no longer operate. Juan explains: 'We used to buy unwanted trucks and trailers for the value of their tyres alone. People knew my name from racing, so I wasn't just anybody from the country when I offered to buy from them. Since they knew of me and where they could find me they were prepared to accept a cheque. That was very convenient for me, and we were backed by the local potato growers because they were doing quite well and we could pay them a better return on their money than the state-controlled banks. We had a reputation for being straight, and during that time it certainly paid off.'

Immediately peace returned in 1945, the economy began to recover. Argentina earned billions exporting grain and beef, and although little of that new found wealth passed on to the general population, 'things' were improving. Now the hauliers all wanted to buy trucks, and Fangio began supplying them. 'I went into partnership with Hector Barragán, the Balcarce Studebaker rep, and we bought incredibly cheap but brand-new GMC and Studebaker

trucks as USA war surplus. I went down to Bahia Blanca for two days to demonstrate a four-wheel drive GMC and didn't come back for two years! Business was so good we stayed in the Grand Hotel there – me, Barragán and Janices, and sold from there. Everybody wanted trucks.'

On 24 February 1946, the populist General Juan Domingo Perón became President of Argentina. He set out to promote Argentina's image worldwide, and as a motor racing fan he saw the sport as a valuable promotional tool.

In Europe, motor racing had been revived as early as September 1945 in Paris. For 1946, quite a comprehensive International series of races was held, commencing with the Nice Grand Prix, won by Luigi Villoresi's pre-war Maserati.

In Argentina dirt-track competition was quick to recover, and in 1946 Fangio drove two brief races before becoming totally immersed in his military-surplus truck business. He drove a pair of Model T Ford specials in these dirt-track events, the first on the La Pomona track at San Justo and the other at Tandil. The cars were prepared and owned respectively by Nardi, and by Naranjo.

Fangio and the Model-T Ford.

On the Tandil speedway, April 7, 1946. Around the track in a shower of . . . dust; Fangio giving Naranjo's Model-T Ford a vigorous work-out, its bonnet already long gone.

'Negrita' – the ugly duckling, Balcarce 1990.

For 1947 the ACA planned to invite leading European teams and drivers to race in Argentina during their closed-season of January-February. Of course in Argentina this was the height of summer, and this race series became know as La Temporada, literally 'The Season'.

The visitors, together with the few pre-war GP cars already in Argentina, were known as the Coches Speciales class, while the ACA permitted home-grown Mecánica Nacional single-seaters to compete with them.

Juan was in Bahia Blanca when the news broke. 'Straight away, I telephoned Balcarce and talked to Cavallotti. There was only 15 days to go before the first race. I got him to ask Toto if a 6-cylinder Chevrolet "war" lorry engine we had for sale would fit into a Ford Model T Mecánica Nacional chassis we had in the garage.'

*The strengthened chassis on
'Negrita', 1990.*

That car had been raced by Pepe Renteria with a 'bitsa' four-cylinder Chevrolet engine. Juan thought a 3.9 Chevvy engine would surely make it fly. While he set out from Bahia Blanca on the 450km drive to Balcarce, Toto and Duffard tackled the job, beefing-up the chassis to support that heavy new engine. When Juan arrived, the work was well advanced, 'The engine was so big it ended-up under my legs. We finished it 15 days after my telephone call. It was race day. We tested it around Balcarce in the dark and set off.'

They christened the finished ugly duckling *Negrita*. She was loaded on the garage's '39 Ford truck and rushed to the Retiro circuit at Buenos Aires. Running late, they eventually unloaded *Negrita* and Juan drove her on the road to arrive at Retiro just in time to take a place on the back of the grid. He finished third, and in the Final, third

again. But the new Chevvy engine had overheated badly. Having worked for 48 hours without rest, Fangio slept on the infield while the visiting Speciales raced round driven by the visiting Europeans – Varzi, Villoresi, Platé and 'Raph'.

'Our new car had some problems. The new engine was so deep its sump dragged on the ground. We had to bend the springs to provide some ground clearance. And the Ford's radiator had been large enough for the four-cylinder engine but was too small for the new six-cylinder. We just couldn't find an old radiator big enough, and we couldn't afford to buy a new one. So instead we put a small additional radiator ahead of the original, and when it still overheated we put an extra radiator in the tail with long hoses connecting to the front and added water pumps to circulate the coolant. Two weeks later we raced like that at Rosario.'

There in *Negrita*, Fangio won the unlimited series and raced against the visiting Speciales, finishing sixth behind Achille Varzi's Alfa Romeo 308C, 'Gigi' Villoresi's Maserati 4CL and Oscar Gálvez's 308C. Although Fangio had been beaten by both the Gálvez brothers for the honour of first Argentine driver home, *Negrita* was the leading local car.

Juan laughs about it today: 'Several garages and agencies contacted us wanting to put our car on display. It proved to me that any car is a beauty if it wins!'

Two weeks later, at Mendoza, Clemar Bucci won the Mecánica Nacional track-race series and the Final, with Juan placing second and third. *Negrita* had had some luck, but was not fast enough.

'I was in Buenos Aires when I saw a really good-looking Nacional for sale, called the Volpi. It had an American Rickenbacker engine. By this time I had a good

September 21, 1947. The excellent
Volpi-Chevrolet in the GP
Primavera, Mar del Plata.

Volpi-Chevrolet, Balcarce 1990.

relationship with the Suixtil textile company, which made
and marketed a whole range of sports shirts and gentle-
men's fashion, and they helped me to buy that car. It
handled well but at Bell Ville I found the Rickenbacker
engine lacked power, so we replaced it with a Chevrolet,
and then the Volpi became a very good car indeed.'

He had a lot of success in the Volpi-Chevrolet, and at
Mar del Plata he won the Nacional race and placed fifth in
the Speciales Final against three Alfas and four Maseratis.
Then for the Gran Premio Internacional de Carreteras, he
bought a suitable coupé in Coronel Pringles.

'I bought it from a Chevrolet agent, two weeks
before the Sierra de la Ventana race. We converted it in ten
days and I practised hard over the Sierra de la Ventana-
Pringles section which in the race I won comfortably,
beating both Oscar Gálvez and Fernandino – another good
driver – on their home ground. That I enjoyed.'

The pre-war Carretera double champion was back,
and in great form. He had a new companion to accompany
him in these races, a great enthusiast who would also drive

Faithful friends. To them Juan says he owes it all. Virtually from the start of his career the only way he would ever see his rivals would be to look behind.

Juan's Mecánica Nacional car when offered the chance. His name was Daniel Urrutia.

They tackled the Gran Premio Internacional the following month, soaring above 15,000 feet through the Andes to Santiago de Chile and back. Fangio led on the return leg until his car bogged down as he cut a corner where the road had been freshly widened. He sent Urrutia to fetch a lorry they had passed some way back, and after two hours it towed them out. Juan was tenth completing that Stage, and finished the race sixth overall.

'I then retired from the Mil Millas, and was only third in the Championship. I wondered if I was too old? But no – I had really made a mistake in buying a '39 Chevrolet instead of a more modern one.'

But despite the disappointments of 1947, at least Fangio had shone in a single-seater, and in the new year he would go one better, and race for the first time in Europe.

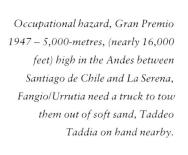

Occupational hazard, Gran Premio 1947 – 5,000-metres, (nearly 16,000 feet) high in the Andes between Santiago de Chile and La Serena, Fangio/Urrutia need a truck to tow them out of soft sand, Taddeo Taddia on hand nearby.

February 1, 1948 – Rosario City GP. Another Fangio first as Juan was invited by the Franco-Italian constructor Amédée Gordini to handle one of these little Simca-based Voiturettes, finishing eighth on the Parque Independencia circuit.

January 17, 1948 – Buenos Aires City GP, Palermo Park, Buenos Aires; Fangio was unimpressed after his first drive in a European-built pure blooded Grand Prix car, the Scuderia Naphtra Corse team's elderly Maserati 4CL...

February 1, 1948 – Fangio pressing Gálvez's big Alfa Romeo 308, in the little Simca-Gordini 1220.

40

1948: Dress Rehearsal

For 1948 the Argentine Temporada series catered for Grand Prix-type cars only, instead of mixing the imported Coches Speciáles with home-grown Mecánica Nacionals. It was announced that the ACA would field a stable of European GP cars for Argentine drivers, and Fangio promptly asked to talk with *don* Francesco Borgonovo, Chairman of the ACA's Motor Sport Committee.

Numerous other Argentine drivers had beaten the same path to Borgonovo's desk. The crucial difference between their approach and his turned out to be that most of them were interested in how much the ACA might want to pay them for their services, while Juan – typically – demanded instead 'How much do I have to pay to drive one of these cars?'

'These cars' were the pre-war style Scuderia Naphtra Course Maserati 4CLs run by Raphael Bethenod de las Casas, better known simply as 'Raph'. Borgonovo's ACA committee selected Oscar Gálvez and Fangio as Argentina's drivers, only for Gálvez to prefer his more powerful 8C-35 Alfa, leaving Fangio to team up with 'Raph'. They faced the Scuderia Milano entries of Farina, Ruggeri and Platé in a 3-litre twin-supercharged Maserati 8CL and a pair of 4CLs. Villoresi also had a 4CL, Varzi a massive 4.5-litre V12 Alfa with 430-horsepower, and Chico Landi an Alfa 308C. Amédée Gordini fielded two 1100cc Simca-Gordinis.

In practice for the Premio Ciudad de Buenos Aires, Fangio set third fastest time, starting Heat One from the front row of the grid on his first appearance in a purebred Grand Prix car. Unimpressed by the car, he still ran second to Villoresi until a pit stop dropped him back to finish fourth. In the Final, he survived only four laps. 'Before getting into that car for the first time, they told me to watch out for all the power when the supercharger came on song,

watch the braking, keep the revs above 3,500 or it would foul its plugs. I felt, it's the same as my Volpi-Chevrolet – and it was! It wasn't even as good, although its gear change was nicer than our's – until the lever came off in my hand.'

A week later Fangio came fifth at Mar del Plata, and Gordini then offered him a drive in Rosario, as team-mate to Jean-Pierre Wimille – the contemporary Alfa Romeo works team's brightest Grand Prix star. Oscar Gálvez and Fangio set the best two times in practice, Fangio lapping $1^1/_2$ seconds faster than the great Wimille in the sister car.

Gálvez led the first 15 laps from Wimille and Fangio in formation, each probing the other's capabilities. Fangio recalls: 'I watched every move he made and decided I could pass him. That circuit was quite tight and twisty, which suited the Gordini perfectly, but my Simca engine had a cracked cylinder head and overheated.' Even so, he set fastest lap. Wimille declared: 'Fangio should be given the chance in a first-class car and then he would surely do great things.' Gordini himself was thrilled and gave Juan a second drive on the 3-mile Palermo Park circuit in Buenos Aires, but there the little French car could only finish eighth, heavily out-gunned on the fast straights.

The Doble Vuelta de Coronel Pringles followed, in which Fangio, accompanied by his enthusiastic friend Daniel Urrutia, won; beating Oscar Gálvez. He then returned to his Volpi-Chevrolet for Mecánica Nacional, winning at Palermo Park and Necochea.

In April he was Carretera racing again, driving the Chevrolet to finish 11th in the Mar y Sierras and then winning the Vuelta de Entre Rios. On 2 May he won yet again in the trusty Volpi-Chevrolet, at Mercédès.

February 29, 1948 – Juan and his co-pilot Daniel Urrutia are feted after victory in the Vuelta de Coronel Pringles race with the Turismo Carretera Chevrolet Coupe.

Partly with all these results in mind, Anesi and Borgonovo and their committee at the ACA had decided it was time for an Argentine fact-finding tour of the USA and Europe. They sent Fangio, Oscar Gálvez and Pascal Puópolo as drivers, ex-driver Ricardo Nasi for YPF and Juan Carlos Guzzi of the ACA. First stop was Los Angeles, then Detroit and the Indianapolis 500-Miles track classic.

Clemar Bucci was already on a European tour, hiring drives from Maserati and Simca-Gordini. They went to watch him race at San Remo on 27 June, where Maserati's star drivers, Ascari and Villoresi, gave the brand-new Tipo 4CLT/48 model its victorious début, finishing first and second. (Bucci was third in an older car.) For ever after, the 4CLT became known as the 'San Remo' Maserati.

The Argentines met the veteran Italian Champion Achille Varzi there, and he invited them to his home in Galliate. Varzi was off to drive for the Alfa Corse works team in the Swiss Grand Prix at Berne the following weekend. Bucci was also entered, and the Argentines went along to spectate. Practice began in steady rain, Bucci

Fangio's first European race at
Reims in July 1948.

crashed, and tragedy struck Achille Varzi. His experimental Alfa Romeo overturned in a freak low-speed accident, and he was killed. The ACA party returned shocked to Galliate for his funeral. On his visits to the Temporada, Varzi had always encouraged Argentine involvement in European racing: now they honoured him for it.

On the telephone from Buenos Aires, Borgonovo urged Fangio to provide a report recommending what racing cars the ACA should order for a projected International tour in 1949. 'Borgonovo told me to say in my report I had already bought one. But a Maserati – which is what we preferred – cost 80,000 *pesos*. I had already discussed such a purchase with my friends at Balcarce, but that was a great deal of money.'

The ACA also appreciated the need for European know-how to run a sensible professional season in Europe. They already knew Varzi's long-faithful mechanic, Amedeo Bignami, so Borgonovo invited him to become the ACA touring team's chief mechanic for '49.

Juan made his European racing debut at Reims. Amédée Gordini met him in the paddock and asked, 'Do you want to drive my car?' Maurice Trintignant had just been badly injured in another crash at Berne, so his Simca-Gordini was free. In Formula 2 practice for the Coupe des Petites Cylindrées, Juan promptly set second fastest time with the 1430cc four-cylinder Simca-Gordini behind Raymond Sommer's 2-litre V12 Ferrari, but he had to retire from the race when running sixth.

In the Grand Prix his car developed ignition trouble, costing him 11 minutes in the pits. Then his fuel tank split, putting him out when he was lying 12th.

Back in Paris on the way home, Jean-Pierre Wimille invited them to the offices of the great French sporting newspaper *L'Équipe* and introduced Fangio as the man who had shown him the way in Argentina in an identical car. 'He is going to be a great Champion,' said Wimille. Knowing Juan, I can imagine him being both delighted and acutely embarrassed by such praise from such a man.

Back home, on 20 October, came South America's greatest race yet. The Gran Premio de la America del Sur ran the length of the continent, from Buenos Aires to Caracas, Venezuela – 5,950 miles to the north in 14 Stages – plus a five-Stage return leg – 3,224 miles more – from Lima, Peru, to Buenos Aires.

For the first time in Carretera racing, the entry was seeded. Fangio and Urrutia started first in their Chevrolet* and were flagged away at 10pm leading 137 other cars at 10-second intervals. It was a madcap race. Roberto Carozzo, in his Fangio book† quotes Gálvez as recalling: 'I gave it everything, and then I saw Fangio held up at the *don* Torcuato level crossing. I pulled up alongside him, revving the Ford. When the train had passed and the barrier went up, we both went off like pistol shots. There wasn't a metre between us. We were door to door.'

This was real motor racing in its purest form – clearly only The Men need apply.

Domingo Marimón led. Fangio was determined not to let him draw away, but after 300 miles the condenser on his Chevrolet came loose. Fixing it lost much time. The final-drive then began to break up. Juan was carrying a replacement crown-wheel and pinion, with a different final-drive ratio, ready for the mountain stages, and tore apart

*Demonstrating the propaganda value attached to racing by the Argentine Government, Eva Perón's Social Assistance Foundation put up prizes of 5,000 pesos plus gold plaques for the two best-placed drivers carrying Peronist slogans on their cars.

†Fangio My Racing Life. *Juan Manuel Fangio with Roberto Carozzo.*

44

Prelude to disaster, October, 1948 – early in the prodigious Gran Premio de la America del Sur, Juan and Daniel Urrutia change wheels and refuel their 'Balcarce' Chevrolet Coupe at the Córdoba control.

In Arequipa, Peru, Juan and Daniel celebrate their victory on the GP de la America del Sur's 5th Stage, 546kms from La Paz, Bolivia. They had just averaged 77.815km/h but their race's tragic end was imminent...

the diff to fit it. But the intended replacement was for a van – it wouldn't fit. Urrutia was beside himself; he had been given the wrong part. So they rebuilt the damaged diff and sent a message to Concepción asking for a suitable replacement to be made available.

Juan lost over four hours on Stage 1. At Salta he started 79th but drove so fast that he finished at La Quiaca fourth, passing 60 cars on the way. Even so his overall position remained poor, and he had to start each successive Stage from that position. 'Every day I had to repass many of the same people I had passed the day before.' He channelled his irritation into driving ever faster.

Halfshafts broke on both the third and sixth Stages – 'I had problems in all the Stages and had to compensate with crazy speed. Poor Urrutia was not doing well. He forgot to prepare one shaft properly before I fitted it and we found a vital component left over after I'd bolted it all back together. I just had to strip it all down and do it again, losing still more time, which then made me drive harder still.'

In La Paz, at the end of Stage 4, Urrutia fitted a blank new exhaust gasket. Juan could hardly believe it: there was no hole in the gasket to allow the exhaust gas to escape. That entailed another strip-down and rebuild, absorbing what should have been time to rest and relax.

Heading for Lima on an 832-mile stage, another halfshaft broke and they were overtaken by their own rear wheel. The following so-called rest day became a furious hunt for spares. They helped rebuild three cars and were scheduled to restart at 5am next morning, but at 8pm that same evening agitated officials warned them to be ready to restart in just two hours' time – a General Odria had rebelled at Arequipa against the Government of President

Bustamente Rivero.

Only 60 of the 138 starters remained in the race, and the restart was confused – some setting off in the wrong order. In the small hours of Friday 29 October the night was foggy and behind Juan came the Peruvian driver Alvarado who should have known those local roads like the back of his hand. Consequently Juan waved him by and tucked in behind to follow. After 85 miles he lay fourth on the road, with Nato Gullé and Oscar Gálvez in the lead. Then Alvarado hit a donkey in the village of Paramanga and overturned. Only Gullé and Gálvez were ahead.

Juan caught and passed Gullé and to shake him off began cutting corners, kicking up dust to add to Gullé's problems in the fog, to deter him from hanging onto their tail. 'Urrutia didn't like me playing dirty like that and asked me not to. That was typical of his good nature.'

Just before Trujillo Juan caught up with Gálvez and passed him. He was in the lead. He recalls: 'I should have stopped at Trujillo for fuel. I was exhausted, it was a terrible strain concentrating hard enough to drive so fast into that awful fog. But I went straight through Trujillo aiming to find fuel at Tumbés, a recognized stopping place.'

A few miles further on, with Gálvez still in hot pursuit, the Chevrolet tore into a village called Huanchasco. Urrutia had just called out: 'In five or ten minutes it'll start to get light.' when out of the fog loomed the stark, white-painted walls of the village. The Chevrolet's headlights glared back from those white walls and Juan was momentarily dazzled as the beams immediately scanned round the next turn into the foggy dark.

He was confronted by a sharp left-hand corner, with inky blackness beyond, apparently a precipice on the outside. In fact it was nothing more than the ground falling

Friday, 29 October 1948 – Huanchasco, Peru. The wrecked but righted Chevrolet Coupe after the dawn accident which cost Daniel Urrutia his life and almost persuaded Fangio to abandon motor racing.

gently away down an embankment, but taken by surprise Juan tried desperately to heave the Chevrolet around the corner no matter what. The car skidded and dropped its right-side wheels off the blacktop onto the sandy verge; they dug in and it began to roll.

'It's a most unhappy memory. I remember clutching the steering wheel to keep myself inside the car. I remember the tools and spares flying around, hitting me. Then all was quiet. The car was lying on its side and I was in a heap against the driver's door with my feet tangled in the pedals.

'Nobody thought much of safety then, but my brother Toto had actually fitted a roll-over cage into that car – the first time we had ever used one. It had held up. We also had safety straps to prevent the doors bursting open, but Urrutia had not fastened them – we didn't like to feel we might be trapped inside. This was fatal, because the doors had burst open as the car overturned and Daniel had been flung out. His neck was broken and if he wasn't dead right then he died soon after.'

Villagers extricated Fangio and toppled the car back onto its wheels. 'Gálvez had seen me turn over and had stopped in a field on the right.' As they got to Urrutia the dawn he would never see began to break.

In hospital at Chicama, Fangio was sedated and slept. When he awoke he found another driver, Manuel Montes, had retired and was keeping him company. (They would later go into business together.) Juan discharged himself and Montes took him to a hotel where they rested for a week. He wanted to rejoin the Gran Premio on its return leg south but Montes talked him out of it. 'I just wanted to test myself to see if I could still do it. Urrutia had been a good friend, I had advised him not to come on that race, but he loved racing and insisted. Tragically he had not seemed to have his mind on the job, perhaps understandably because back in Buenos Aires his wife was about to give birth to their third child. They already had two daughters, and this was a boy – born after his father's death.

'Regardless of the circumstances, no matter how tired we were after all the delays and problems, the accident had been my fault. I thought then of stopping racing altogether. It was hard to bear.'

Automovil Club Argentino Simca-Gordini, Balcarce 1990.

1949: Overnight Sensation

It took some time for Fangio to recover mentally from that traumatic experience. There had been no Mil Millas race in 1948, and when the delayed event was run instead on 16 January 1949 Fangio was out to prove something to himself. Accompanied again by Elizalde, he started 125th and finished second behind Oscar Gálvez – by that time the King of Carretera racing. 'That was by far the dustiest race I ever did. When we finished the car was full of it, and we were chalk-white from head to foot.'

On 29 January, the Temporada series began, and the ACA team's newly-delivered Maserati 4CLT/48s faced the European threat. Fangio and Andrea Malusardi were entrusted with the new cars, while Benedicto Campos drove an ex-Villoresi Maserati with the older body but a similar engine. The visiting 4CLT drivers included Villoresi, Ascari, 'Bira' and Reg Parnell, while Farina had a 2-litre V12 supercharged Ferrari.

During early-morning practice at Palermo Park on 28 January, Wimille crashed his Simca-Gordini and was killed. Despite this the race went ahead. For Heat One, Fangio and Malusardi joined Ascari and Villoresi on the front row. Juan ran second until a right-rear tyre burst. 'There was no tyre of the right size in the pits so I had to fit two smaller ones, which left the car so badly under-geared I had to lift my foot to stop the engine over-revving on the straight.' Gálvez finished third and Fangio fourth.

Mar del Plata was like a hometown race, only 35 miles from Balcarce where it seems the only man in church that Sunday was the priest. Juan led the race – and all the foreign stars – from start to finish, despite being deafened by a broken exhaust. Sadly, Malusardi crashed fatally in practice.

Back in the Volpi, Juan won twice more before

The ACA's Equipo Argentino Achille Varzi Maserati 4CLTs with Fangio and his 1949 European tour team-mate, Benedicto Campos.

leaving for Europe to lead the ACA's new touring team. The Equipo Argentino was well equipped and well supported, but though Europeans tended to think of Argentina as a money-rich nation which had escaped all the ravages of war, the ACA team's budget was very tight. It was up to Fangio, who played an important part in team management, to attract extra support.

He visited Pirelli in Milan and asked them to grant him tyres on account. 'Until we had earned some start or prize money we couldn't afford to pay for any, and Pirelli were very helpful. That's why, when they asked me to come to London for the launch of their book *With Flying Colours* in 1987, I agreed to come immediately – to repay that old debt.'

Also in Milan he found a small oil company named 'Lubra', which he approached for oil at a special price. 'Lubra was a vegetable castor oil and the company was run by Francesco Corvella. He listened to our proposal and agreed to give us free oil as long as we painted the Lubra

Juan greatly respected Alberto Ascari but the Argentine media made much of bad blood between them when Fangio first shone in Europe in 1949, and both Ascari and his countrymen like Villoresi objected to what they wrote. Juan's diplomacy detuned the media-men and he and the Italian stars became firm friends.

Juan and the Duke and Duchess of Windsor at Jean-Pierre Wimille's memorial service after the great driver's fatal accident in a Simca-Gordini in Buenos Aires, 1949.

The Italo-Argentine team's European HQ was at Galliate in the province of Novara and here are Fangio, friends and team-mates with one of the trusty – but tired – Maserati 4CLT engines at the garage there, with ACA-liveried Simca-Gordini Voiturettes or 'Formula 2' cars on the left.

name on our lorry and wore Lubra-lettered caps and overalls. He also offered us 150,000 *lire* for any race we managed to win. I don't think he believed there was much chance of that. Neither did we but that was good money.'

The team made its European début at San Remo. The first day's practice was inauspicious. Fangio's engine ran a big-end. Back in the garage, he dropped the sump and repaired the damage himself. Not until 1am raceday did he tell the mechanics to finish reassembly – he was going to bed.

That afternoon he won the first Heat and trailed 'Bira' to the finish in Heat Two, to win comfortably overall on aggregate time. His logical approach, expending the least effort necessary to win, was all part of keeping the Equipo's hardware together for the longest European season possible. And Signor Corvella of Lubra owed the Equipo its first bonus.

After a break the Equipo was off again – to Pau in France. Juan led handsomely there until his engine ran out of oil near the finish. He called at his pit to top up and two litres were being added when an official made him switch off the engine. He had tried to keep it running because the Equipo had no auxiliary electric starter, and push starts were forbidden. The flustered mechanics tugged at the starting handle, then Bignami began to lift the bonnet to fit new hot plugs. Seeing his lead ebbing away, Juan rushed round to the nose of the car, shouldered aside the mechanic on the handle and wound the engine carefully onto compression. One smart upward tug and the motor fired. He hopped back in and tore away to win, with Campos third.

Another minor French race followed – the GP de Roussillon at Perpignan – and Fangio won again, beating 'Bira' as at San Remo with Campos third again.

Marseilles saw the third race of the French series, and another win for Fangio – by that time the sensation of the season. This time he drove a Simca-Gordini, better

April 3, 1949 – San Remo GP, Ospedaletti circuit, Italy – Juan is about to make his European come-back in the ACA Maserati and will win both Heats and the race overall on aggregate. Over the following three months he would win five more European races.

suited to the circuit even though the fast straight saw him being badly buffeted in practice by the airstream. Bignami obtained some perspex, which they fashioned into a wrap-around windscreen to replace the normal small 'aero' type. Juan was careful not to fit it until race morning in case the opposition thought it was a good idea. He finished second in Heat One, while Campos won Heat Two and in the Final Fangio was never headed.

'After that win Signor Corvella at Lubra owed us 600,000 *lire*. I was sure he'd never pay up, it was such a small company. I went to see him – he was out. I went to see him again – he was out. I went to see him again – and at last he was in. He greeted me very warmly and congratulated me on our success and paid up and we became friends.'

For the Rome GP at Caracalla, Juan was badly advised. An Argentine friend persuaded him to run a 2-litre sports Maserati instead of the Simca-Gordini, and it broke a piston after an unhappy race.

All the Equipo's personnel were mighty impressed by the unsupercharged 2-litre V12 Ferrari single-seaters which shone at Caracalla. Fangio called Borgonovo to ask if anything could be done about buying two of the cars. I suspect that while the ACA's own budget was tight, both Juan and Borgonovo had a pretty shrewd idea that further backing could be obtained from the Government now that the team had proved itself a winner. In two short months it had done wonders for Argentine prestige in Europe.

While this request was being considered, the trucks lumbered north to Spa for the Belgian GP, only for Fangio's Maserati to break a piston in practice and a valve on lap 2 of the race. The hard-used 4CLTs were desperately in need of a factory rebuild, so the new Ferraris were vital.

May 22, 1949 – Marseilles GP, Parc Borely, First win for Fangio in the Formula 2 Simca-Gordini.

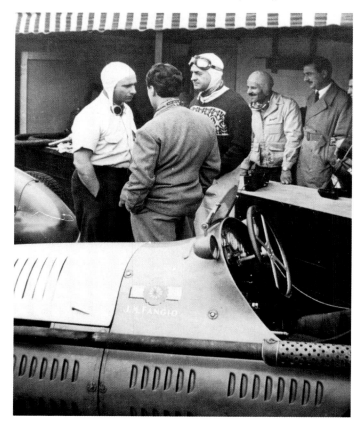

June 19, 1949 – Belgian GP, Spa– Juan's second Grande Epreuve after the French GP of 1948 but his first in a fully-fledged Formula 1 car, the Maserati 4CLT with Andre Simon, Louis Rosier, and team-mate Campos behind the pits.

THE MONZA ILLUSION

Fangio was doing well in Europe in the Spring of 1949, but the races he'd won had been relatively small-beer events, without entries from the top team of the day – the works Ferraris, handled by the formidable former Maserati pair of drivers, Ascari and Villoresi. Their cars had run in the Rome GP at the Baths of Caracalla, and Villoresi had won there hands-down.

The next event in which the Argentine Equipo would meet the Ferrari team head-on would be on 26 June in the Monza Autodrome Grand Prix. This was a Formula 2 event for unblown 2-litre cars, not to be confused with the annual Italian Grand Prix for Formula 1 cars which was traditionally held at the same circuit in September.

After broaching the subject of acquiring a Ferrari with Pancho Borgonovo of the ACA, Fangio apparently received a telegram assuring him two cars had been ordered and were ready for collection. Borgonovo and President Anesi of the ACA were in Europe for the annual meeting of the International governing body, the FIA, and they met their men in Milan and all travelled together to the Ferrari factory at Maranello. They were all excited, because the news was that the Government was buying the new V12 cars to ensure the national team's continued success.

At the Maranello works they found two new single-seaters, ready to go, but one in primer and the other painted Italian red, not in the Equipo's Argentine pale blue and yellow as expected. The reason was blunt: the ACA had not yet paid for them, and the price was $11,000.

Borgonovo and Anesi apparently knew the Club could not afford to settle such bills, but meanwhile Juan had telephoned a friend in Government service in Buenos Aires to find out exactly what was going on. 'He told me to be very careful I didn't make a mistake and buy the team a car which couldn't win. I assured him that if I had such a car I could win all right.'

On the understanding that the payment was on its way, one car was released to Juan three days before the race. 'I ran it in at the Modena Autodrome, but there was trouble with the gearbox which the factory didn't seem able to fix. It wouldn't select fifth gear.'

After Monza practice, the works Ferraris were wheeled out ready to take their places on the grid but the car intended for Fangio was impounded, silent, in the paddock garages. The story goes that Ferrari told Borgonovo and Anesi they would only release it if one of them signed an irrevocable letter of credit on behalf of the ACA. Neither was empowered to do any such thing, but if they didn't then Fangio would have been left without a drive.

The broadcasting brothers, Luis Elias and Manuel Sojit, had established a listening audience of millions tuned in to Radio Belgrano back home, avidly following their reports of the Equipo's successful tour of Europe. Everybody back home had heard the team was to run a new Ferrari in the Monza race, and the loss of Club credibility if Juan did not start was too awful to contemplate.

So the two officials took a flyer and wrote out an IOU on the pit counter, without any authority to do so from the Club they represented, and the car was promptly handed over. While the ACA men sat on the pit counter, chewed their finger-nails and wondered what on earth they had let themselves in for: 'The race became a battle between me and the Ferrari works drivers, Ascari and Villoresi. I

The Automovil Club Argentino Ferrari 166 America, Balcarce 1990.

couldn't get fifth gear at any time and in fourth the engine was really shrieking away at 7,500rpm along the straights. It was fortunate Ferrari had fitted long gearing at the factory, otherwise it would have been impossible.

'After the scheduled pit stop I went all out to try to catch Ascari and I was closing fast when I realised the cockpit was so hot my legs seemed to be burning. The oil temperature gauge was almost off the clock. All I could do was lift off to rest my engine, because I still could not find a higher gear. Then I saw Ascari stationary in the pits, and only Bonetto was ahead of me. I was also troubled by vibration which turned out to be broken spokes in the rear wheels. We only had two spare wheels and they didn't have the stronger spokes fitted into the set on which we started. I could not afford another pit-stop, so I just nursed that car round, lifting my foot along the straights. But still all the oil was burned away, there wasn't much water left and I finished with the engine absolutely ruined.

'That was an incredible win for me – it just seemed an illusion that an Argentine could actually win at Monza!'

Ferrari later charged the Equipo an extra 300,000 lire for repairs – which really did have to be paid before the car was again released for Juan's use at Reims. Borgonovo and Anesi were let off the hook: funds were at last forthcoming to honour their IOU, reputedly from Alberto Dodero, a wealthy supporter of General Perón. Juan's great victory against Ferrari's finest at Monza had won the day. In time for Reims, at last, the first car was repainted in Argentine national racing colours and it, and its sister, subsequently enjoyed a very long and successful racing career far south of the Equator.

December 18, 1949 – Gran Premio
Juan Domingo Peron, Palermo
Park, Buenos Aires – No mistaking
the crowd's partisan reaction as
Fangio yowls by in the ACA's
supercharged V12 Ferrari en route
to second place.

The Maserati engines were rebuilt at Modena and the 4CLTs then whisked to Albi in southern France. There, 'Bira' cracked a block in practice and Juan – typically – gave him the Equipo's only spare, to Bignami's intense disgust. Next day Fangio beat Bira's rebuilt car to win yet again. Trailing northward, the Equipo arrived at Reims the following week. For the Formula 2 tace there they unloaded a Maserati and the repaired Monza-winning Ferrari.

During practice, the Maserati began running on only three cylinders. Inspection revealed a damaged valve-seat. Bignami despaired, but Fangio insisted he could fix it, and he did just that, working with only the most basic equipment in the local GM dealership.

In the race Juan drove the Equipo's Ferrari and dominated the event until his gear-selector fork snapped.

Money was still tight. The Equipo even slept in the trucks so that money for hotel bills could be devoted to the cars. Whenever they could wangle it they ate free, and at the end of the season Juan's precise accounts were readily approved by the ACA back home.

There, the motor racing fans who sat glued to their radios listening to the reports from Europe had been thrilled by his success. Five great wins in the Maserati, one in the magnificent Ferrari – all fantastic news.

On 25 August 1949 Fangio landed at Móron Airport, Buenos Aires, returning home as a national hero to a State reception. It was the first of many such triumphant homecomings from the European battlefield.

On 5 November he started his last big Carretera race, the Gran Premio de la Republica, covering 6,856 miles in 12 Stages around Argentina. He started between Oscar Gálvez and his brother Juan, and won Stages 2, 7 and 9, but: 'Juan Gálvez drove very well and I just did not feel at home any more on those dirt roads. I was badly out of practice in that kind of racing.' He finished second, splitting the Gálvez brothers, who thereafter had Carretera racing virtually sewn-up between them.

Ageing disgracefully – but undeniably original, one of the ACA team's Formule Libre Ferraris as rediscovered and offered for sale by Christie's in 1990.

FANGIO – THE MAN

I consider Juan Fangio to be so much more than just the greatest driver I ever raced against. To me these things are arranged in pyramids. A pyramid rises to a point and in my personal league-table of the great drivers I raced against, the man who stands on that pinnacle entirely alone is Fangio.

Just below him in terms of ability I would place Jimmy Clark and Alberto Ascari, both approximately on a level. But Juan had everything. He had an unreal level of natural talent and ability, allied to a quite remarkable temperament, and yet he was much more than just one of the most outstanding sportsmen of his period. He was and he remains a most extraordinary human being, and the acid test of that must be a simple question: How many other men of such achievement were thought of in their time, and are remembered universally today, with such abiding genuine affection? I can think of precious few.

Fangio is extremely sociable, but he doesn't seek people out. Yet if invited he will most happily and comfortably be absorbed into any company.

Is he a man's man? Well, he's undoubtedly attractive to women but it would be demeaning to describe him merely as a ladies' man. In fact he's a broader personality than either of those glib terms. He is a people's man and during the forty-odd years that I have known him, he always has been an extremely attractive personality.

He is very much a man's man without being macho. There's no display about him. He has always been a kind, caring person – a simple man, without in any way being merely simple.

He is blessed with great genuine warmth – while at the same time has enormous strength of character. He is not

hard, yet not soft, a man with so few flaws it hurts.

He was an outstanding practical mechanic, but never a theorist in technical terms. During his works team career in the World Championship years he never fiddled around with his cars in any attempt to make them more capable. He would always simply drive them as they were. In effect, the only way he could improve a car was by driving it so much better than anyone else.

He is a man who breeds confidence in those around him, because he is a confident man. Following him at racing speeds when we were teamed together for Mercedes-Benz certainly gave me enormous confidence. But he doesn't display any of this and he never has. He simply is it. I never worried about following him, no matter what he might do on circuit – it just would not have occurred to me to have the least doubt in his judgement.

If you are going to be good at motor racing, you have to have that confidence. During the 1950s, if a team had Fangio on their side then they had a head start over any rival which rubbed off on the mechanics and on the engineers and throughout the entire organisation. He had then, and he retains still, an immensely charismatic presence which inspires all those around him. And yet he has always remained an enormously accessible person.

Because neither of us speaks the other's native language, communication between us on a more than superficial level has always been somewhat arm's length. He's not an earnest racing enthusiast. Very few drivers of our era were at all interested in discussing racing between themselves and Juan and I were no exception. But I regret that in the time we raced together we could never discuss on a psychological level the philosophy of racing, and the finer points of the art we both practised with such success.

At Mercedes I spent perhaps more time with the chief engineer, Rudi Uhlenhaut, and my fellow driver Hans Herrmann, because they both spoke English very well. But if there was any practical joking going on, or a good party, Fangio was always ready to join in the fun. He was never a ringleader in that sense, but he'd always join in for a lark most readily, and his girlfriend of the time, Andreina, was always around with her ready smile. They didn't socialise with the rest of us young lads as a couple, but they had a kind of warm and friendly presence which we appreciated on the rare occasions they appeared with us together.

As multiple World Champion, Juan bore his responsibilities most conscientiously – the responsibilities one has to one's team and to one's sport. For example the pressures upon him to drive at Monza in 1952, the day after racing the V16 BRM in Ulster, were absolutely huge. Against almost impossible odds he made it to that race, and the after-effect of his efforts damn near killed him.

Perhaps the respect in which I and my peers all held him during the period we all raced together are best exemplified by the way in which Peter Collins handed over his Lancia-Ferrari to Juan for him to finish the Italian Grand Prix at Monza in 1956, and thereby also surrendered his chance of becoming World Champion in Fangio's place. I think Pete felt that if he had helped The Old Boy to achieve what he deserved to achieve, then that was the right and proper thing to do. So he did it willingly, and he has always been remembered nobly for it.

That's a similar thing to the day in New Zealand when my Cooper had broken a half-shaft and Jack Brabham lent me one of his. In the race which was to follow, Jack knew I was probably the only person who could beat him, yet he still lent me that half-shaft. And in the race I beat him.

Pete was like that. When we drove as team-mates for Aston Martin he stepped down and gave me his car at Rouen because it had drum brakes which on that course I preferred to my own Aston which had discs. He and Jack did those things for me, and in similar circumstances I'd like to think we would all have done them for Fangio.

I can't think of any facets of Juan's character which one wouldn't like to have in one's own. And on top of all this he was so quick . . . So do you appreciate now why we should have compiled this affectionate tribute to motor racing's great Champion? It's because he, in so many ways, deserves every word of it.

January 15, 1950 – Fangio leading
Ascari's works Ferrari before
trouble struck in the Mar del Plata
City GP on the seaside El Torreón
circuit. It was here on the beach
that he would later play soccer for
hours under the mid-day sun to
build his fitness and legendary
stamina.

July 9, 1950 – As a fully-fledged
Alfa Romeo factory driver, Fangio
shows Farina how in the
non-Championship Bari GP. It was
during this race that his good
humour left an indelible impression
upon the young Stirling Moss.

1950: First Love – Alfa Romeo

During 1949, the new Ferrari marque had been able to dominate top-level Grand Prix racing while Alfa Romeo's hitherto all-conquering works team took a sabbatical. The Portello company's reasons for temporary retirement were twofold. Financial times were hard, but they had also lost their three great drivers, Varzi and Wimille in accidents and Count Trossi in hospital to lung cancer. With assistance from their dealers and also from their long-time supporter and tyre supplier, Pirelli, Alfa Corse then planned a comeback in 1950. Dr Alessio, their director, was looking for the world's top drivers to replace the stars he had lost. Consequently, he signed-up 'Nino' Farina and the veteran Luigi Fagioli, a man who had driven before the war for both of the great German teams – Mercedes-Benz and Auto Union.

To join them – and to create Alfa's famous 'Three-Fs' team of drivers – Alessio then selected Juan Fangio. He had seen Juan's first sensational win at San Remo in 1949 and had followed his subsequent career with increasing interest.

Alessio offered a contract for the Grand Prix series of Formula 1 races which in part that season counted towards the FIA's newly instituted World Championship of Drivers, but otherwise left Juan free to drive any cars he wanted in events which Alfa Corse did not enter.

Before returning to Europe to take up this fabulous offer, Juan drove in four Temporada races back home, all in the ACA Ferraris. He particularly remembers Rosario: 'I was in the lead and came round to lap Bonetto in a corner but he hadn't seen me and moved across, so to avoid hitting him I went off over a roundabout and crashed straight into straw bales around a column. Of course we had very poor

flag marshalling then. There were no flags to warn a driver he was being overtaken, and that taught me a lesson. It is important to have the best machine. But when you have the best machine it is equally important to be patient. There is no need to be in a hurry to overtake your rivals. To finish first – you must first finish.'

He was back in Europe by 19 March when he finished third at Marseilles in the ACA Equipo's Ferrari 166. Then on 10 April he won the Pau GP again in their faithful Maserati 4CLT.

His Alfa Corse debut followed on 16 April, in the non-Championship San Remo Grand Prix. The team had entered two *Alfettas*, one for Farina and what was regarded very much as 'the second car' for Fangio. But Farina had broken his shoulder at Marseilles, and Alfa agonized over whether to scratch both San Remo entries rather than rely entirely upon their new driver. It was a difficult decision, since they were defending such a long unbeaten record and this was their comeback race.

Juan recalls: 'I still hadn't signed any contract, and they really wanted to pull out of the race, but I was obviously keen to take my chance, so I told them "Look, if I lose, it's Fangio the unknown driver who loses, not Alfa Romeo. But if I win it's Alfa Romeo who wins, providing an unbeatable car for the unknown driver."'

They swallowed it. He tried his car briefly in a rainswept practice session, lost time at the start with wheelspin but fought his way through to the lead after 13 laps, and then led comfortably to the finish. 'Engineer Colombo asked me if I had an automatic gearbox! Alessio wanted me to sign the contract afterwards in the hotel but said first we have to agree what money you want? I just signed, and told him to fill in the noughts. I think they were very surprised, but I thought that was right. They were the greatest Grand Prix team in the world and they were giving me the chance to drive their fantastic cars.'

I know exactly how he felt. We both raced for the love of it, the money was completely incidental. The only way we would afford to go racing was to be paid to do so, but the numbers were largely irrelevant, being handled in my case by someone else.

The following Sunday saw Juan driving for Alfa Romeo in his first Mille Miglia.

Alfa Romeo 159 reunion – Fangio and his former Pirelli racing department tyre fitter Mauro Povia, south of France, 1990.

April 23, 1950 – Alfa Corse put
Fangio straight into the Mille Miglia
in only his second drive for them,
sharing this 6C/2500 Berlinetta
Sperimentale with mechanic Zanardi
to finish third overall.

FANGIO'S FIRST MILLE MIGLIA

The Mille Miglia – Italy's great classic thousand-mile road race out from Brescia and back again – was an awesome point-to-point blind on everyday roads closed for racing.

'After San Remo, Dr Alessio wanted me to drive in the Mille Miglia and they entered me in a 2,500 six-cylinder. To keep me company – because it was lonely up in the hills if you got stuck – they gave me a mechanic named Zanardi as passenger. But the day before the race, we went to get the car from the factory and it wasn't available. It turned out that it had been sold to a Signor Bornigia who was going to sell Alfa Romeos in Rome. Next day we went to Brescia not sure whether we were going to race or not. Alessio went off for a long talk with Bornigia and returned all smiles. We were ready to race.

'I had hardly had any practice at all in the car and didn't know anything about it. I had to rely upon what Zanardi told me. I don't think he felt very confident in me. He knew I had no experience of the Mille Miglia at all but he knew the route quite well. The cockpit was so noisy that conversation was utterly impossible, so he said he would slap his hand once on the dashboard for a corner which was a little danger, twice for a corner which was a big danger and three times for a corner which was deadly!'

From my experience of being navigated by Denis Jenkinson in the Mercedes-Benz 300SLR during our winning drive in the race in 1955, it seems to me that just for once Juan had this the wrong way round. The deadliest corners needed the shortest warning signal, not the longest.

However, Juan continues: 'Before we set off I asked Zanardi what rev limit I should use. "Five thousand," he said. So I kept to 5,000 revs for the first part of the race until the service depot at Pescara. Then, near Popoli, Bonetto went past in a big 4.5-litre Alfa Romeo and Zanardi – I think he had more confidence in me by then – screamed "Five thousand five hundred revs!"

'By this time we were really racing and I pressured Bonetto until his engine broke and then in the mountains near L'Aquila it began to rain and I slid in a corner and when I regained control after quite a long slide I was so pleased I let out a great whoop and then noticed Zanardi grinning at me. He told me later, my whoop convinced him he was riding with a wild Indian from the Pampas!

'The car had been too hastily prepared and its windscreen wipers did not work. It was already night when we got back to Modena and with the rain and spray and no windscreen wipers I could hardly see a thing. Then Cortese passed us in his British Frazer Nash, which was an open car: he could look over his windscreen and had a good view, so I tucked in behind and followed him, right on his tail. And he led us all the rest of the way to the finish at Brescia.

'I was pleased to finish third in those circumstances, and it gave Alfa Romeo more confidence. For me that first Mille Miglia was an important race, but it was hard – the Mille Miglia was always hard.'

May 13, 1950 – The British GP
inaugurated the new Drivers' World
Championship. It was 'Royal
Silverstone' as King George VI is
introduced to Alfa Corse's legendary
'Three Fs' team – Fangio, Farina
and Fagioli, with guest No 4 Reg
Parnell extreme right.

May 21,1950 – Monaco GP, composed, intent, Juan powers his victorious Alfa Romeo 158 through the Tabac Corner where his perception saved him from a disaster which embroiled half the field . . .

On Saturday, 13 May the inaugural World Championship of Drivers was launched in the British Grand Prix at Silverstone. It marked bitter disappointment for Fangio: his *Alfetta*'s engine failed. But the following Saturday saw round two – the Monaco Grand Prix.

For that season, Alfredo Pián and José Froilán González were the Equipo Argentino's two new drivers. Pián had finished third at San Remo, but he crashed heavily in Monaco practice and broke his leg. Juan was exceptionally fast and started from pole while González qualified on the outside of the front row, with Farina's *Alfetta* in between.

On the first lap, Fangio led Villoresi's Ferrari but in the quayside left-hander at Tabac, Farina spun, clouting the stone steps. Fagioli spun into him. González struck both Alfas glancing blows and bounced them apart, before accelerating away towards the Gazométre hairpin. As he

braked for that corner, fuel sloshed forward from the filler cap which had sprung open just behind his neck. The spray ignited on the exhaust and he was lucky to escape with serious burns to his neck and shoulders.

Meanwhile, back at the Tabac, seven more cars had become involved and the corner became a chaos of crumpled cars, gushing fuel from ruptured tanks. Miraculously it did not ignite.

Down towards all this mayhem at racing speed came Fangio and Villoresi. 'That became a fine example of the good luck which accompanied all my racing days. The evening before the race I had been looking through the Monaco club's photo albums. There were shots of a similar collision in the 1936 race, at the chicane. Coming down towards the Tabac I was forewarned by seeing the backs of the crowd, instead of their faces. I thought "Oh, something

69

more interesting than the race leader around that next corner'', and the pictures of that 1936 accident came into my head. So I managed to stop centimetres from the nearest crashed car. To get through I reached out to grab its left-rear wheel and eased it back and opened a gap just big enough to weave my car through.

'Villoresi had managed to stop just to the right of me but he was badly blocked, so I was away! After that nobody could catch me, even when I stopped to refuel, and so I won my first World Championship Grand Prix.'

After the race, Juan pulled the front seat out of his 'issue' Alfa road car to accommodate a stretcher on which he drove Pián – with his broken leg in a cast – to the specialist Istituto Rizzoli orthopaedic centre in Bologna. Two days later he was back in Monte Carlo, this time in the Equipo's Suixtil-supplied Chevrolet, to chauffeur the burned González to a specialist Italian burns clinic in Novara. He might be a fast-developing superstar, but his heart would always remain as big as a house.

Farina having triggered this first lap 'carambolage' at Tabac, his Alfetta (32) is parked tail-first against the wall (foreground), while Rosier's Talbot (16), de Graffenried's Maserati (52), the Gordinis of Manzon (10) and Trintignant, Harrison's ERA, Rol's Maserati and Schell's Cooper all piled up behind – Villoresi's Ferrari (38) was badly blocked next time round as Juan accelerated clear, while it was also route barrée for Chiron's Maserati (48). With alcohol fuel flooding the track from ruptured tanks, Juan (34) raced on while the ERA and Rol's Maserati were eventually prised apart and parked with the other wrecks – including Farina's against the stone balustrade . . .

Juan raced twice for Alfa Corse in Switzerland during 1950, retiring from the Championship Swiss GP at Berne in June but winning the GP des Nations at Geneva in July. Here with mechanic Zanardi at Berne.

Through that busy summer of 1950 he drove in 13 more races on successive weekends. For the ultra-tight Circuit des Ramparts race at Angoulême on 11 June, the Equipo fitted a six-cylinder A6G sports car engine into one of the 4CLT/48s, to allow that F1 car to run in unblown Formula 2. In blistering 40-degree heat – in the shade! – Juan's car jumped out of gear at the start. He then drove like a madman (his words) to regain ground. When he took the lead on the tiny little circuit around the city walls, he

still had 110 laps to go! He was grateful for someone who drenched him with a bucket of water in a hairpin corner – and he won.

In the Championship Belgian GP at Spa, the race was Juan's, for he beat his team-mate – and arch-rival for the inaugural World title – Nino Farina.

Juan then accepted Amédée Gordini's invitation to drive a tiny 1490cc *Berlinette* in the Le Mans 24-Hours endurance classic. He was partnered by González, recovered from his burns, but the little car stood no chance: 'Gordini was a very clever man. He appreciated years before almost anybody else that what counted was power-to-weight ratio, not outright power in a car weighing whatever it happened to weigh. But for Le Mans, such a very fast circuit, a car like the Gordini with good power-to-weight but little outright speed was like a fish out of water. We drove the poor thing so hard it could not stand the strain – it just went WHEEEEEEE! all the way round, and revved itself into retirement.'

It was at Bari that I first realised not only what a fine person Juan was but also appreciated his outstanding skill. As I wrote in my introduction, I was driving the HWM there, and during practice. I was standing behind the straw bales on the exit to one corner, watching him and Ascari practising. Both were, of course quite outstanding. Ascari was drifting out to within one inch or so of the bales, sliding just so far and no farther, lap after lap. But then Juan would come sliding out of the same corner and he would brush so close to the bales that the protruding stalks would quiver, and one or two might break and fly off. And he would do exactly the same, lap after lap. He was as consistent as Ascari and was using just that tiny fraction more road to go just that tiny fraction faster. And it was

August 15, 1950 – Drama near the finish of the Pescara GP assigned-winner Fagioli's Alfetta is crippled with front suspension failure and Fangio glances across, briefly undecided whether to pass . . .

fractions such as that which made the difference between a very great champion, and an absolute genius.

Juan won the non-Championship Grand Prix des Nations at Geneva on 30 July. Fagioli was scheduled to win his home-ground race at Pescara but near the finish his *Alfetta*'s suspension broke and Juan drew alongside, only for Rosier's Talbot-Lago to threaten to pass them both. So Juan signalled he was taking off to protect Alfa's unbeaten record, and he did. That day, the 158s were timed at 193mph along the Montesilvano straight.

The World Championship would be decided at the Italian Grand Prix at Monza on 3 September, with the title lying between Fangio and Farina. Juan was favourite as he qualified on pole position and began a prudent race, planning simply to trail Farina and await developments. But Alberto Ascari was driving the latest 4.5-litre unsupercharged Ferrari V12 and he began a fierce duel for the lead with Farina. Juan watched the race develop until Ascari retired and '. . . then I was about to make my effort when a tyre burst. After a pit-stop, steam began filling the cockpit.

I think the radiator had been punctured. I took over Taruffi's car, but it broke a valve and that was the Championship lost.'

Even so, second to Farina in the inaugural World Championship was no disgrace at all. Again he was received joyfully in Argentina, where he won three quick races in a row – two in the ACA Ferrari and the other, the Rafaela 500-miles, on dirt in (of all things) a Talbot-Lago!

It had been quite some year, but 1951 would be his most spectacular yet.

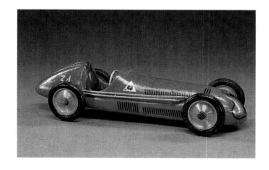

Rare curio – After clinching their second consecutive World Championship at the end of 1951, Alfa Corse presented this 1:10-scale Alfetta – autographed by drivers Fangio, Farina, Fagioli, de Graffenried, Sanesi and Taruffi – to Director Alessio. It was offered for sale by Sotheby's, London, in 1990.

73

1951: Campeón del Mundo

In Argentina by this time, Juan Fangio was the motor racing name to be conjured with. In January 1951 he opened his new business, a Mercedes-Benz dealership and YPF fuel service station in the capital, Buenos Aires, situated on the corner of Bernardo de Irigoyen and Cochabamba.

The new Temporada season saw Buenos Aires' traditional venue in the Palermo Park replaced by a new road circuit beside the Rio Plate – the Constanera Norte.

Amidst great excitement the Mercedes-Benz factory team was to reappear for the first time since 1939, fielding revived pre-war Type W154 Grand Prix cars in slightly modified form. These immensely powerful machines used 3-litre two-stage supercharged V12 engines and 'to make a better competition of it', the ACA – abetted by Fangio – he confesses, decided to shorten the straights on the Costanera Norte using chicanes to give their own 2-litre supercharged V12 Ferraris a sporting chance. This promptly backfired on Juan, as he was invited by Mercedes' famous roly-poly racing manager, Alfred Neubauer, to handle one of their cars as a team-mate to Hermann Lang and Karl Kling, and it was González who beat all their 'silver arrows' in the nimble ACA Ferrari.

Fangio finished third in the Premio Ciudad de Buenos Aires on 18 February and retired from the follow-up Premio Eva Perón the next weekend.

Some maintain that a month later, he was back in Europe, retiring the Equipo's Maserati from the Pau GP in his last appearance in the car in which he had made his name, but he did not in fact race there.

Out in the *Alfetta* again at Silverstone for the BRDC International Trophy, he won Heat One and World Champion Farina the second. The Final was then drowned out by a torrential rainstorm after only six laps.

He was out of luck in the ACA Ferrari at Monza and in a Simca-Gordini in Paris, but on 27 May the new World Championship opened with the Swiss GP at Berne. Juan started from pole position and led through heavy rain until his scheduled refuelling stop, rejoining five seconds behind Farina but soon reeling him in and pluming past to win.

'That win in Berne was very important to me, for a strange reason. The night before the race I took my road car round the track with a couple of friends to really memorize the track down to the very last detail. And suddenly a black cat shot out of the bushes in front of me and I ran straight over it. My friends began joking about how unlucky it was to kill a black cat but I have never been very superstitious and although I would prefer it had not happened I was not too bothered. But next day it was raining. The Berne track had always been quite dangerous, whether it was wet or dry, and I could not forget that this was where Varzi had

Juan at speed in the Alfa Romeo 158 during his victorious circumnavigation of the Bremgarten, 1951 Swiss GP. None was his equal in such conditions.

July 14, 1951 – British GP, Silverstone. This full-strength Alfa Corse team fought a desperate rearguard action against the burgeoning Ferrari team; left to right, drivers Consalvo Sanesi, 'Nino' Farina, Felice Bonetto and Juan Fangio, with team manager/test driver GiovannBattista Guidotti.

June 17, 1951 – Belgian GP, Spa. Juan's almost Nordic calm utterly belies his Latin heritage during the interminable pit stop which put him out of the Championship points.

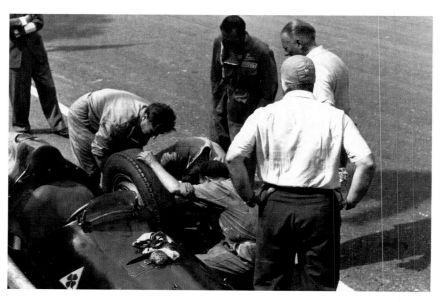

been killed in the rain – in an Alfa Romeo – three years earlier. And the spot where the cat ran out was the place where the previous year my car had broken a valve when leading with 13 laps to go. And at Silverstone when a valve had also broken, there had again been 13 laps to go. If I had been superstitious, surely I would have given up right then! But no rational person should become enslaved to superstition, you have to ignore it, and I won that race – black cat or no black cat. That was an important lesson.'

In the Belgian GP at Spa, Farina beat Ascari's Ferrari by three seconds after Fangio lost 14 minutes in the pits when his left-rear wheel jammed on its splines during a

July 14, 1951 – British GP, Silverstone. One of Juan's greatest attributes was his ability to share lesser or younger drivers' joy when they actually managed to beat him. Here Froilán González has just inflicted Alfa Corse's first real defeat by the new marque, Ferrari.

scheduled tyre change. Juan impressed everyone with his utter calm as he stood quietly by and watched his lead evaporate. His mechanics had to fit a brand-new hub assembly, and he eventually finished ninth.

For his second Le Mans, he shared a factory 4.5-litre Talbot-Lago with Louis Rosier. They ran as high as second only for the scuttle oil tank to split, gushing hot oil over the driver's legs. They did their best to struggle on, but it was hopeless.

The French Grand Prix followed, at Reims. Ferrari's latest 4.5-litre unsupercharged V12 cars were pressing the highly supercharged 1.5-litre straight-eight *Alfettas* ever harder. Previously the thirsty *Alfettas* had been so blindingly fast between refuelling stops, they could easily regain any time lost against the bigger, slower, but more economical, unblown cars. But the modern Ferrari V12s clearly matched the *Alfetta's* top speed and for much of the race they could run lighter than the Alfas which were bloated with fuel away from the start and after each refuelling stop.

At Reims, Juan duelled wheel-to-wheel with Ascari's

Ferrari, until his *Alfetta's* fuel pump failed. Fagioli was signalled to bring in his car to hand it over, and while Juan was waiting, Ascari retired. González was making his debut for Scuderia Ferrari and he was called in to hand over to Ascari. Eventually Juan won in Fagioli's *Alfetta* from Ascari in González's Ferrari.

The British Grand Prix followed at Silverstone on 14 July, and before official practice began Juan drove Froilán round the aerodrome circuit in his Alfa Turismo, these good friends comparing notes. Despite driving Ferrari's oldest 4.5-litre *muletto*, González promptly dominated practice to qualify on pole position and the race became a battle royal between him and Fangio. 'We passed and repassed and I was in the lead when I had to refuel. I did not need a tankful but the pit-staff topped it up anyway, which made the car too heavy for me to catch Froilán again, and so I finished second and Ferrari had beaten Alfa Romeo for the first time. They were very happy, and I was very pleased for Froilán – winning his first World Championship Grand Prix.'

For the German Grand Prix at Nürburgring, Ascari selected the muletto Ferrari in which González had won at Silverstone – and it won again. Fangio remembers: 'That was the first time I had seen the Nürburgring. I loved it from the first day. It was a fantastic challenge, and I drove round it lap after lap in my 2.5-litre Alfa road car to learn it all. I tried to learn it section by section, and tried to remember in particular the fast parts, because the slow sections were like driving through the mountains which I was very accustomed to doing. At that speed there was usually a margin for error, to compensate for a mistake, so you just drove by eye, while in the really fast sections there was no margin for any error, any mistake or confusion would be severely punished, and that was where careful practice and knowledge of the course really could pay off.'

During practice he was caught out, entering a left-hander too fast, missing an emergency down-change and spinning tail-first into what he described as 'a mound of earth' which stopped him running over the verge into the ever-present trees. He qualified third fastest and admits he was in a foul mood, most unhappy with his car's clutch and gearbox. It was stripped and reassembled that night but was no better next day. The clutch failed as he left the startline, and since only third and fourth gears would then engage cleanly he confined himself to those two for the duration. He managed to set fastest lap, and to lead the race, but the inoperative clutch made restarting tricky after the pit-stop and he stalled. After eventually being restarted, he finished second, Ascari winning Ferrari's second consecutive World Championship qualifying round. Alfa Corse's old invincibility was a thing of the past.

Juan's explanation for that clutch trouble is interesting: 'It was discovered that the groove in the flywheel in which the clutch-spring is meant to seat was not deep enough. What happened was that after the initial acceleration, as I de-clutched, the spring popped out of its groove and from then on I had no clutch.'

His was the only *Alfetta* to survive that race. Something clearly had to be done at Portello or Ascari and Ferrari would steal their Championship.

The minor Formula 1 race at Bari provided light relief. Against Ascari's Ferrari, Juan found his Alfetta had a slight advantage over the circuit's twisty section but Ascari had the edge on speed along the straight. It had become Juan's custom to explore his car's capabilities to the extreme in practice. Having decided the latest possible point at which he could brake into the 90-degree right-hander ending the straight at Bari, he was braking consistently earlier in the race until he decided Ascari had come quite close enough behind him. On that lap he suddenly left his braking absolutely as late as he dare and Ascari – taking his cue from the *Alfetta*'s tail – was drawn far too deep into the turn and was taken completely by surprise. Locking his brakes, he promptly spun while Fangio teetered round. Although the gearbox seized in fourth gear, Juan won comfortably.

Two weeks later, the Italian Grand Prix at Monza saw three Alfas retire and only Farina survive to finish third behind the triumphant Ferraris of Ascari and González.

'Some people in the factory were fired after that amongst suspicions of sabotage – the fuel filter in my car, fuel tank in Bonetto's, refuelling problems too.'

Amidst considerable tension, therefore, Alfa Corse prepared for the climax of that season, and of the second Drivers' World Championship – the Spanish Grand Prix at Barcelona. They put around the story that extra pannier

*July 28, 1951 – German GP. Juan is
push-started in the Alfetta during
his fraught first acquaintance with
the majestic Nürburgring – six years
later the stage for his most fabulous
performance.*

*Drivers can be valued by the
regard of their mechanics –
no mistake here, Fangio
and Zanardi.*

*Fangio at Nürburgring could not
quite catch the Silverstone-winning
Ferrari, which won again but this
time in Ascari's hands.*

October 28, 1951 – Juan's tyre-change stop during the World Championship-deciding Spanish GP on the Pedralbes circuit, Barcelona, which the Alfa management had kept secret even from him until he was on the starting grid.

Somewhere amongst this scrum on the Pedralbes pit apron are the winning Alfa Romeo 159, new World Champion Juan Manuel Fangio, and Dr Alessio, his elated employer at Alfa Corse.

fuel tanks fitted for that race would enable their latest *Tipo 159* cars to run non-stop. In fact they would inevitably have to refuel over such a distance, but Fangio was not told just in case he might let word slip to his friend González at Ferrari. Only when the race was about to start did Colombo tell him: 'Fangio, you'll have to make a stop'.

'On my car and Farina's the foot-level air duct was not for the feet but to feed the superchargers. They told me not to open it until the traffic had thinned a little and the dust had been blown from the circuit. For the first ten laps then, I kept this duct shut, and when I opened it I felt sure I was going to win because the car went off just like a rocket.'

Juan trailed Ascari closely, pressured him into leaving an opening and dived ahead. Ferrari had been tricked entirely into believing Alfa were attempting to run non-stop 'and that's what really persuaded them to fit small 16-inch wheels and tyres against our 18-inch. I saved my tyres all the time, sliding not at all. I don't think they even had to fit new tyres to my car in the pits. If Ferrari had known we were going to stop they would have used the larger tyres and beaten us but we were much faster on the straight for the first time that season and that was how I won in Barcelona – and won my first World Championship.'

After the disappointment of so narrowly losing the World title in that last race of 1950, he was now Champion of the World – for the first time. His reception that year in Buenos Aires and Balcarce alike was more deliriously ecstatic than ever before – and it was so well deserved.

November 1, 1951 – 'Whoever wins the title pays the bill – the loser chooses the restaurant and invites the guests!'. This was the bet between Fangio and Ascari at Barcelona, and here they are at their 'marvellous party' for 40 or 50 in Milan's Ristorante Savini, Galleria del Duomo. The choice was Italian, the bill settled by the Argentine . . .

Spanish Grand Prix Trophy, 1951.

Alfa Romeo 159, south of France, 1990.

March 23, 1952 – Juan winning for the fourth consecutive time in the ACA's 2-litre supercharged Ferrari 166C America at Piriapolis, Uruguay. It was a great start to what proved to be his most disastrous 'season'.

1952: Disaster

March 16, 1952 – Premio Eva Perón, Autodromo 17 de Octubre. Juan Manuel Fangio and his young friend and rival José Froilán González, after yet another of Juan's wins in the ACA Ferrari.

Eva and President Perón with Fangio. Buenos Aires.

Having narrowly won the 1951 World Championship with Fangio to add to the inaugural 1950 title with Farina, Alfa Corse bowed to financial restraints plus the increasing obsolescence of their *Alfetta* and quit Grand Prix racing for 1952, while at the top.

Omer Orsi – who owned Maserati – invited Juan to lead his team in the new season's Formula 2 races, which the FIA were about to elevate to World Championship status. Juan readily agreed, while through Argentina's British car importer – Eric Forrest Greene – he also arranged to drive BRM's much-publicised new V16-cylinder car in European Formule Libre and Formula 1 events.

During 1952, Juan drove in only twelve races, of which he won six – all in South America – including a string of five consecutive victories.

In the first three months of the year he drove only the ACA's Ferrari 166 America single-seaters, starting with a Brazilian tour in which he won at São Paulo and Rio (Boa Vista) but retired from the incredible 'Devil's Springboard' road race on the Gavéa, Rio's traditional racing circuit. Back home he then won the first two races run at the new purpose-built Buenos Aires Autodrome. Two races followed at Piriapolis, across the River Plate in Uruguay, and his ACA Ferrari won them both.

He then returned to Europe and made a guest appearance at Easter Monday Goodwood, where he drove a misfiring new Cooper-Bristol into an unhappy sixth place on the day that a tall young blonde boy named Mike Hawthorn launched his career with three wins in a sister car.

Three weeks later it was the serious business of his second Mille Miglia with Zanardi, this time in an Alfa

Romeo 1900 touring car. They finished 22nd.

June was to be a busy month, Juan making his BRM debut at Albi on the 1st, driving for them again the following weekend in the Ulster Trophy at Dundrod, and then rushing to Monza overnight for his first race as Maserati number one. At Dundrod I was to be his team-mate for BRM, having spent much of the previous winter testing their intended new 'world-beater' at Monza. It was undeniably fast, but otherwise quite dreadful. I had made a long list of recommendations to improve it, but few of them had been seriously listened to.

Of course BRM had made a terrific song and dance about signing-up the reigning World Champion. He and González had visited their test-centre at Folkingham Aerodrome near Bourne in Lincolnshire. Trying the V16 there for the first time Juan was hugely impressed with its fantastic power, and its absolutely ear-splitting noise! But even his remarkable skills were hard pressed to control the car when its centrifugal supercharger kicked-in the power and it took off with runaway wheelspin. He went off over the grass and tore off an exhaust stack on a hidden runway light.

When BRM's people — headed by Raymond Mays and Peter Berthon — asked how he thought their car could be improved, his apparent response was typical: 'What's the matter? Wasn't I quick enough? If your car goes slowly, change the driver.'

I don't entirely agree with that attitude, because I firmly believed in trying absolutely everything to make your car technically capable of going faster. You might then find some advantage, and give yourself an easier time. But it speaks volumes for Juan's remarkable humility, and his ability to make difficult machinery shine.

At Albi he set fastest lap before the BRM's engine failed. They then had to rush the two cars to Dundrod and they simply were not up to it. The engines there were in a terrible state, and the narrow, yet very fast and demanding country-road course at Dundrod magnified the chassis' handling deficiencies. I retired early after coming round one corner on the opening lap to find Juan facing back towards me, having spun his V16 as 'Bira' flew through a hedge in his hefty OSCA. That was the first time I ever overtook Fangio in a Formula 1 car — only thing was that his was going backwards at the time! I was relieved to retire and Juan packed up soon after. But he was faced with a real problem — because 'Bira' had agreed to fly him to Monza in his private plane, but after his early incident the Siamese Prince had left on his own. Fangio was stranded.

He really was in a terrible fix. Accompanied by Louis Rosier, he eventually caught a scheduled flight to London, but failed to find a connection to Milan from there. He flew on with Rosier to Paris but the weather had closed in and onward flights were cancelled. They then checked the train timetable — no joy either. Around midnight Rosier offered to drive him to Lyons in his Renault. There might be some kind of flight available from there. They left Paris in the height of a terrible storm and arrived at Lyons just after dawn. Again no flight, so Rosier lent Juan his car and the World Champion hurtled on over the Mont Cenis pass, wearing Rosier's tyres to the canvas.

As he puts it, 'I arrived at Monza at two, I was in the Maserati on the grid at half-past, and I was in hospital by three.'

The ACA mechanic Bernardo Perez had the Maserati

June 7, 1952 – Ulster Trophy, Dundrod. Fresh from Fangio's first experience of the V16-cylinder BRM at Albi, the cars still looked good but were under-prepared, unreliable and for Moss, Juan's team-mate for the first time, just undriveable on the narrow country roadway. It was still a fabulous-looking car.

– one of the new 2-litre 6-cylinder A6GCM models – waiting for him, and the other drivers and organisers had agreed that he, as the reigning World Champion, could start without practice from the back of the grid. In essence that was fine by him, he knew Monza like the back of his hand. As he tells it: 'I passed six cars on the opening lap and was going well on the second. Heading into the second corner at Lesmo, I got my line wrong and I touched the low barrier on the inside, the car began to slide and instead of correcting it early I let the slide develop, my instant reaction being that I would correct it later on the left side of the road. But due to fatigue this instant reaction was wrong.

June 8, 1952 – Monza Autodrome GP for Formula 2 cars. Disaster after Juan's heroic overnight dash from Dundrod in Northern Ireland, when he crashed his brand-new Maserati A6GCM on the second lap here at Lesmo. He was initially feared for, but his damaged neck vertebrae eventually healed with the aid of this body cast. While he never regained full freedom to turn his head he was cured of a recurrent headache problem following long, hard races.

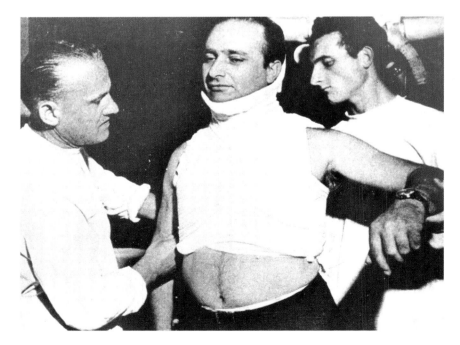

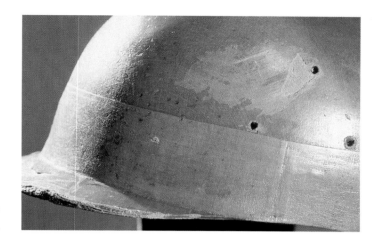

Fangio's then-new crash helmet scarred in the Monza crash.

'I hit the very last of the line of straw bales on the outside of that corner. They had been there for years and alternate rain and sun had baked them like stone. When the Maserati struck I was astonished – it instantly flipped. I remember gripping the wheel tight and then my grip being broken and flying through the air towards the trees. I remember smelling grass, and then I lost consciousness. I was wearing a crash helmet – as required by the new regulations that year – and I later found it had a big scrape across one side and the peak was damaged. It had clearly saved my life.'

But he had still been badly hurt, cracking several vertebrae in his neck, and injuring his left thumb, presumably when his grip on the steering wheel had been broken. He had for some time been troubled by terrible headaches after a long, hard race, none worse than after the Spanish GP only eight months earlier. At the time he had put it down to holding his head up against the 185mph airstream on the long Pedralbes straight, but now as the Milanese doctors carefully X-rayed his neck they found an old lesion and nerve damage almost certainly sustained in his 1948 Peruvian crash in the Chevrolet.

As it was, they put him in traction for six days, then plastered him from waist to neck, locking his torso and head into total immobility for twelve weeks until 3 September, when the cast was removed and physiotherapy could begin. He recovered without paralysis, despite losing some mobility in his neck which left him ever after noticeably tending to turn his shoulders to turn his head, and with a slightly displaced left thumb. But never again was he bothered by those terrible headaches – every cloud has a silver lining.

As he says, he learnt his lesson: 'I had been in two bad accidents, one in Peru and then this one at Monza, and the common factor in them both was my fatigue. Never again, not even on everyday roads, would I ever drive when I felt tired. If I did not feel absolutely fit and ready to go I would just stay put, or find a hotel and stay the night. I had learned my lesson the hard way.'

He was unable to race again before the start of the new year, and his World Championship passed undefended to Alberto Ascari of Ferrari. But for Juan the overriding compensation was that he was at least alive – and he would return.

1953: From Comeback to Carrera

Fangio returned to racing in 1953, in what proved to be his busiest season. He drove in 24 events; won five of them and finished second no fewer than eight times. Like so many others after a heavy accident, he took some time to recover dominant form. That wasn't perhaps so much a reflection on him personally, as on his circumstances. He was driving mainly for Maserati in Formula 2 and while their latest A6GCM model was one of the most handsome of all front-engined racing cars, it lacked the power to beat Ascari's dominant Ferraris.

Juan's first race after the Monza crash came on 18 January 1953 in the Buenos Aires Autodrome. He was running second in the works Maserati when its propeller shaft broke, fortunately flying downwards, not up! Then, in the Buenos Aires City GP, more mechanical trouble left him to finish ninth. The annual pilgrimage to Europe followed, and opened with a classic Mille Miglia.

April 26, 1953 – Mille Miglia, Italy. The lovely looking Alfa Romeo Disco Volante Berlinetta in which Fangio and Sala finished second with only one wheel steering.

May 3, 1953 – Bordeaux GP, France. Fangio finished third in the latest 2-litre 1987cc Gordini, the French 'Sorcerer' now operating independently of Simca backing.

April 26, 1953 – Race organizer
Renzo Castagneto with Fangio
immediately after his incredible
drive into second place in the
one-wheel steering Alfa Romeo
Disco Volante Berlinetta.

ONE-WHEEL STEERING

In the 1953 Mille Miglia, Juan was entered by his first love amongst European racing teams – Alfa Romeo. They had prepared for him a handsome and potent 3.6-litre Disco Volante Berlinetta, and he took off from Brescia accompanied by Giulio Sala, an Alfa Romeo experimental department mechanic of whom he thought highly.

This was Juan's first race in Europe since his Monza crash, and he staged a typically polished performance to prove he had lost none of his old controlled skill and daring. He was second at Rome, though well ahead of Mille Miglia specialist Giannino Marzotto's 4.1-litre Ferrari when, on the mountainous stretch between Florence and Bologna, his car suddenly lurched towards the verge.

'What had happened was that the chassis itself had broken just where the steering box was mounted, and as I wound the steering from lock-to-lock so the broken support tube moved around and allowed the steering box to "think for itself!" I found that when I steered to the left it went where I wanted, but when I steered to the right it would only really go straight on. At the Bologna service depot I asked the mechanics if they had electric welding and they said "No," so I said "OK, close the bonnet," before they could look inside and see exactly what had happened. I was afraid that if they saw it they would surely make me retire. Neither did we want the officials to look inside and see the broken chassis, or they might make the decision.

'So I drove on, keeping well down to the right of the road camber where I had the best chance of getting round the right-handed corners. Bridges were the most dangerous thing, because I had to take aim on them from a long way back to ensure we met them between the parapets.

'Salita was just as keen as I was to continue – he was ideal company in such a race. One problem was braking, because if I tried to brake too hard the load on the broken front end would make that right-front wheel turn outwards. So I tried to use the brakes as sparingly as possible, and relied instead upon changing down through the gears so that the rear wheels did the work, and that minimized the weight transfer effect towards the front.

'Of course we were losing time all the way, but at last we drove into Brescia, and it was only on the very last corner that the car went straight on in a right-hander and I hit the straw bales. I had to reverse, but we drove on across the finish and we were placed second behind Marzotto. I was quite happy to have finished when we should surely have been forced to retire – but I would rather have won it without such drama!'

May 31, 1953 – Albi GP, Les Planques, France. Lining-up the V16-cylinder BRM on pole position ready for the car's best-ever display, winning Heat One from Ken Wharton's ill-fated sister car.

September 26, 1953 – The noise went round and a'round and came out here, in this case just beneath Juan's right-elbow on his last appearance in the V16 BRM.

Back at Albi on 31 May he renewed his association with BRM's ferocious V16. In 1953 they had completed a lot of development work on both the engine and the chassis, and at Albi, Juan demonstrated the car's potential, and also some of its enduring faults.

Recalling the V16 at Albi '53: 'The BRM was really difficult to get off the line, because below around 7,000rpm there seemed to be no power at all but at 7,200rpm there was so much power and torque it was almost unbelievable. I was fastest in practice, and for the Heat I lined up the car on the very edge of the track where the road was quite dusty and loose. That way I could get the wheels spinning and when the tyres gripped I was off as if from a catapult!

'I left Ascari and Farina way behind and broke the lap record. It was the most fantastic car I ever drove – an incredible challenge in every way.'

And when he says that he still shakes his head.

'In the Final I was in the lead and accelerated out of the village at the end of the circuit along the narrow straight, lined by dozens of enormous trees, on the way back towards the corner opening onto the short pits area. Now I don't know why I did it, but something about braking into the previous corner must have felt strange, because I pressed the brake pedal in the middle of the straight, and it flopped straight to the floor – I had no brakes at all! If I had not tested the brakes like that I would next have needed them entering the tight final right-hander before the pits and the trees on the outside there – whoooo!' – he arches his eyebrows and flings his arms wide – 'This *biiig!*'

'A wheel-bearing had broken which displaced the disc brake caliper. Of course then we had no twin hydraulic circuits and so with one caliper not working the car had no brakes. My luck, you see.'

Juan after his record-breaking Heat win at Albi. His car would strip its tyre treads in the Final.

I'm sure he's being modest again. There's a fine line between luck and the product of experience, sensitivity and a kind of sixth sense which the very best drivers have all possessed. A similar thing happened to me at Silverstone in 1959, again on a BRM – in that case a 4-cylinder 2.5-litre P25 model – and an indefinable 'something' about the way the brake pedal felt at Woodcote Corner led me to brake early for the next corner. Sure enough – there was nobody at home, but I had enough room to spin it to rest just short of the safety bank.

Juan drove the BRM three more times that season, at Silverstone and Goodwood, posting two second places and a retirement. Meanwhile he shared an Alfa Romeo coupé at Le Mans with Onofre Marimón – Domingo Marimón's son, who was a very promising young Argentine driver – but they retired with piston failure. The same fate befell Juan and Consalvo Sanesi in the Spa 24-Hours in July, but then at Merano for the Supercortemaggiore race on 6 September he ran an open cockpit Alfa Romeo Disco Volante and won handsomely. Gianni Lancia also invited him to drive for Lancia Corse, in the Nürburgring 1,000kms and right at the end of the season in the legendary Carrera PanAmericana open road race through Mexico.

The rest of the time he drove for Maserati, but the A6GCM, even in its latest rebodied form with that ever-improving six-cylinder engine, was never quite reliable enough to beat the all-conquering Ferrari 500s, though it was certainly fast, as Fangio and his team-mate González proved in the Belgian GP until first Froilán's car failed, then Juan's. Juan took over the Belgian Johnny Claes' sister car and on the last lap was closing on Villoresi's Ferrari for second place, when he uncharacteristically crashed.

'That was my own fault. It was not fatigue. Froilán's car was parked at Stavelot and I pulled out at very high speed to go round it. I went off the normal line onto slippery gravel scattered across the road, and despite everything I could do, my car slid off into the ditch and threw me out. I thought it was going to topple over on me, but it poised above me – and then fell back onto its wheels.'

He escaped with bruises and was back in harness again in time for the French Grand Prix at Reims. That was Mike Hawthorn's great day when he drove brilliantly for Ferrari and beat the Maseratis of Fangio and González to become the first British driver to win a Grande Épreuve since Dick Seaman – for Mercedes – in 1938. I was British Racing Green with envy, but I had been trying hard to go Grand Prix racing in a competitive British car and in truth at that time there was simply no such animal.

Mike battled with Fangio for 32 epic laps and described it like this: 'We would go screaming down the straight side by side absolutely flat out, grinning at each other, with me crouching down in the cockpit, trying to save every ounce of wind resistance. We were only inches apart, and I could clearly see the rev counter in Fangio's cockpit. Then once, as we came into Thillois, he braked harder than I had expected and I shunted him lightly, putting a dent in his tail. That shook me... I thought it would take some living down. But he showed no resentment at all; he just kept on fighting every inch of the way, according to the rules, in the way that has earned him the admiration and respect of everyone in motor racing...

'I had a totally unexpected bit of luck. As we swung into the last lap, it suddenly dawned on me that Fangio had not changed down into first gear for Thillois. Perhaps he was having trouble with the gearbox. Last time we were only inches apart as we braked, changed down and down again. Then I slipped into first, the tyres gripped; I gained the precious yards I needed and I was leading by a second as the chequered flag came down.'

That was a great win for Mike but I have always thought that just for once Juan had made a tactical mistake in allowing him to get clear on that last lap. I couldn't understand why he hadn't just sat on Mike's tail and slipstreamed past the Ferrari on the final run-up to the flag.

But it had been a wonderful race, and a great result for our new generation of British drivers. Ascari promptly

July 17, 1953 – Practice for the British GP, Silverstone. The Maserati mechanics push-start Fangio in the latest A6GCM Formula 2 Grand Prix car. Chief Mechanic Guerrino Bertocchi wears his favourite leather jerkin and cap. Juan will finish second in the race, for the fifth time that season.

July 5, 1953 – French GP. Fangio at Thillois corner, where Hawthorn beat him.

August 23, 1953 – Swiss GP, Bremgarten, Berne. Waiting coolly for the start with French photo-journalist Bernard Cahier and the Maserati mechanics. By the end of the day he will have scored yet another second place.

September 13, 1953 – Italian Grand Prix, Monza. Most important race of the year and victory at last for Maserati in the handsome A6GCM/53 after a last-corner pile-up on the second Curva in Porfido being entered here, sidelined Ascari (Ferrari '4') , Farina (almost hidden behind him) and Onofre Marimón (Maserati '54').

September 6, 1953 – Supercortemaggiore GP, Merano, Italy. A win at last, in the works' latest Alfa Romeo Disco Volante Spider after preferring it to the standard closed Berlinetta; 'visibility was far superior and I had an easy drive'.

slapped us down again by winning the British GP, with Fangio second, Farina won the German GP, with Fangio second, and Ascari won the Swiss GP, with Fangio second yet again. Throughout the summer of '53 it was a remarkably consistent pattern, Ferrari beating Maserati.

Juan recalls: 'That was to be my first race at Monza since the accident. The season had been Ferrari's all the way but we had been pressing them harder with every race. The problem at Monza was that the four-cylinder Ferraris had a lot of torque which enabled them to come out of the corners quicker than our six-cylinder Maseratis, even though we were going faster by the time we approached the end of the straights. Unfortunately the finish line was closer to the exit of the Porfido curves than it was to the end of the straight, so if we were all together on the last lap the Ferraris would have a great advantage on the final acceleration towards the line. I spent much of practice trying to find the quickest line out of the last corner, and I was ready to take my Maserati to 9,000rpm and blow up if necessary just as long as it got me to the finish line first.

'Final practice worried me because my car had a terrible vibration. Guerrino Bertocchi, Maserati's chief mechanic, assured me it would be fine next day, they'd work all night to put it right; and in the morning, it was.

'I started from the middle of the front row, between Ascari on pole position and Farina, both in Ferraris. Marimón was in another Maserati on the second row and he joined in with our group. It was a great race, with us all slipstreaming each other in a bunch right up until the final corners. There were two right-handers there in those days, with a short straight between them, and on that last lap Ascari was leading Farina, who was pressing very hard. On the second of the Porfido Curves Ascari began to spin. Farina went onto the grass to avoid hitting him, but Ascari slid back into Marimón's path and they collided. Again my luck carried me through. I had aimed for the inside and as Ascari slid backwards so a gap opened right in my path and I went through to cross the finish line first.

'The organizers were so astonished that the group had not appeared all in a bunch as before, they did not show me the chequered flag and so I did an extra lap at racing speed to make sure I kept ahead of Farina.

'But I had won the Italian Grand Prix for Maserati, and Omer Orsi was in tears he was so happy. So far Ferrari had won every race, and the public was on our side as the underdogs. When we won at Monza their reaction was wonderful.

'The funny thing came later when I asked Bonetto – who was also in our team – how his race had been. He said he was pleased still to have teeth in his head, because his car had vibrated so much! I realised then that what Bertocchi had done to cure that problem was to swop my car's numbers with Bonetto's!'

Juan added to Maserati's joyful September by beating Ferrari again in their home-town Modena GP, and then in November came the Carrera PanAmericana – for Lancia.

He spent October in Balcarce, then flew to the USA where General Motors loaned him a Chevrolet to study the Carrera's 1,912-mile route. Lancia believed the powerful Ferraris would surely dominate the final, straight and level Stages after Mexico City, so they planned instead to attack on the first three Stages which combined flat plain with twisty mountain sections. The Carrera comprised eight

Italian Grand Prix Trophy, 1953.

Stages run over five days and on the very first Stagnoli and Scotuzzi of Ferrari were killed and six spectators died when struck by an American sedan.

Bonetto won that Stage, followed by his Lancia team-mates Taruffi, Fangio and Eugenio Castellotti – with Umberto Maglioli, the leading Ferrari driver, fifth. On the Puebla Stage, Taruffi beat Bonetto, with Fangio third once more. Into Mexico City, Taruffi won again, cutting Bonetto's overall lead to 40 seconds. Juan had an off-road moment and lost more than five minutes when oil spilled from an unclipped filler onto the rear tyre and he spun. He limped the final 60 miles into Mexico City where in three hours the Lancia mechanics replaced the entire rear end.

While they worked, Fangio and Bonetto drove on for a final recce of the next Stage's opening miles. Juan had already left some Argentine-blue and white paint markers as personal warning signs. Some led into a series of very fast curves entering a village named Siláo, in which a series of gullies crossed the road. He apparently pointed these out to Bonetto, but next day the veteran Italian either forgot or ignored them in his duel with Lancia team-mate Piero

September 20, 1953 – Modena GP, Italy. Two home wins in a row and this time in Maserati's home-town; Juan with his team-mate and protégé Onofre Marimón (left) and industrialist Adolfo Orsi, owner of Fratelli Maserati SpA.

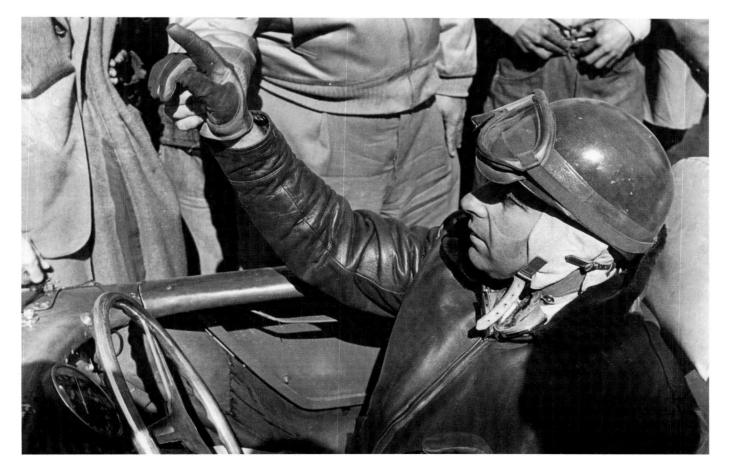

November 1953 – Carrera PanAmericana, Mexico. Seated in his victorious, beautifully prepared, exquisitely built and very fast Lancia D24 Spider.

November 19, 1953 – At Oaxaca, Juan has just finished third in the opening stage of the Carrera PanAmericana. He will not win a single Stage, but will accumulate outright victory with the fastest time overall as days later the three surviving works Lancia D24s cruise across the finish line, 1-2-3 (Below).

Taruffi – who was catching him rapidly.

In fact Taruffi had already over-cooked it and left the road on those deceptive fast curves leading towards the village. He was just staggering back onto the tarmac with his steering bent when Fangio came by and entered the village itself. There he was greeted by the sight of Bonetto's shattered Lancia. When he reached Léon, a small boy told him that Felice Bonetto – his great friend and team-mate – had been killed.

Maglioli won that Stage for Ferrari. Taruffi fought back for Lancia to win the next, to Durango, while Fangio, deeply upset, paced himself carefully towards the finish in his wake. Overall he held a ten-minute lead over Taruffi, with Castellotti third on aggregate, another eight minutes down. To Juan's alarm the team seemed intent on risking everything to beat Maglioli's Ferrari in the final Stages. Poised for an outright victory, he felt that was madness. He advised they should all forget Maglioli, because he stood no chance of victory overall, and should concentrate instead upon restricting themselves by 500rpm to complete a crushing team victory.

'I told them I wanted above all that Lancia should win, but if my team-mates attacked my lead I would go all out to defend it.' Pasquarelli, the team manager, checked with Gianni Lancia and agreed that plan, and against Fangio's preference to drive alone – mindful of what had happened to Daniel Urrutia – a mechanic named Bronzoni was detailed to accompany him as insurance against any last-minute mechanical problems in the leading car.

While Maglioli won that final Stage into Ciudad Juárez at an average of 138mph, the three Lancias roared

Carrera PanAmericana – After Bonetto's death, following those of the Ferrari crew Stagnoli/Scotuzzi on the opening stage, this was a cheerless victory.

across the finish line in team formation, Fangio winning the race overall from Taruffi and Castellotti. It had been a great triumph for Lancia Corse, though marred for everyone by the death of Bonetto.

At least it was a victorious end to what had been an important and busy come-back season for Fangio. Now a new 2½-litre Formula 1 beckoned, with promise of an all-new Grand Prix car from the most illustrious marque in motor-racing history – Mercedes-Benz.

January 17, 1954 – Argentine GP, Buenos Aires Autodrome. Juan being heartily congratulated by President Juan Perón after his great home win in the brand-new Maserati 250F. This was the opening race of the new 2½-litre Grand Prix Formula

January 31, 1954 – Buenos Aires City GP. A rare occurrence back at the Autodrome, again in the works 250F, as Juan was out of luck, and retired.

1954: From Maserati to Mercedes-Benz

As both a World Champion driver and a Mercedes-Benz dealer, Fangio was an obvious choice to be selected as team leader for the giant German company's return to Grand Prix racing in 1954. Their new 2½-litre Formula 1 cars should have been ready for the first round of the European World Championship at Spa – but they were delayed until the French Grand Prix, at Reims. Meanwhile, Juan continued to drive for Maserati.

The Italian team's new 250F cars made their debut in the Argentine Grand Prix at the Buenos Aires Autodrome on 17 January. The straights there were too short for the 250Fs' new 2½-litre six-cylinder characteristics, and Juan hoped for rain to negate Ferrari's power advantage. His new car was exceptionally well balanced, and on raceday the rains came after he had been demoted to fourth place by three works Ferraris. He retook the lead on the slippery track – lost it as the course dried – and then another torrential storm broke. 'The sky was black as night. My goggles misted up and I took them off and was almost blinded by rain drops striking my face like stones. I signalled I was coming in and when I stopped they gave me a visor and fitted rain tyres,* and then I was able to catch Farina and Froilán to win.' Sounds simple, doesn't it?

Two weeks later in the non-Championship Buenos Aires City GP he retired early. At Sebring for the 12-Hours sports car race he shared a Lancia with Castellotti and again retired. Then on 20 June in the Belgian Grand Prix at Spa, Farina and Hawthorn rushed into an immediate lead. Juan slipstreamed past them on lap 3. Farina pulled out all the

*There were no 'rain tyres' in the modern sense at that time, merely standard tyres with extra tread sipes cut in them to increase water drainage

The formidable figure of team
director Neubauer signals from the
pits. Here Fangio and Kling are
running 1-2 with a 15 second lead.

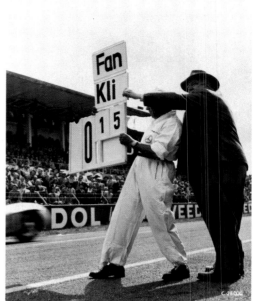

July 4, 1954 – French GP, Reims-
Gueux. The mighty Daimler-Benz
Rennabteilung's return to Grand
Prix racing saw Juan immediately
qualify his glittering new
Mercedes-Benz W196 'streamliner'
here on pole position, flanked by
German team-mate Karl Kling –
both of them overshadowing
Alberto Ascari (Ferrari '10').

stops and repassed until smoke streamed from his Ferrari's exhaust and he dropped out. Fangio was bothered by high water temperature but was able to ease back and the temperature levelled. His car's radiator had been punctured, and he won with the engine so badly cooked its spark plugs were welded into the head!

After the Supercortemaggiore race at Monza in which Juan retired a 250S sports shared with the universally popular Onofre Marimón, Mercedes were ready. That first fuel-injected, all-inboard braked Mercedes-Benz W196 was fully streamlined, fantastic to look at and difficult to drive. In its early, long-wheelbase form it understeered terribly at high speed and Juan subsequently asked the German engineers for a version with hub-mounted front brakes to provide some extra front-end 'bite'.

He won the French Grand Prix handsomely from his new team-mate Karl Kling. Then in the British Grand Prix at Silverstone the new cars seemed terrible. Juan explains: 'With that wide streamlined body, with the wheels hidden from view, I could not judge the corners well because Silverstone, being an airfield circuit, was very wide and the corners were marked by old oil drums. On the entry to the corners I found myself maybe only a few centimetres off line, but that meant at the apex of the corner maybe half a metre off line and at the exit perhaps a whole metre. It made a terrific difference. The track was also damp and slippery, and I finished fourth with the body of my car badly battered against those marker tubs.'

Kling narrowly ahead in his 'Stromlinienwagen' as he and Juan storm along the narrow straight between the Reims pits and main grandstand at around 150mph.

July 17, 1954 – British GP, Silverstone. Drum-roll at Beckett's Corner as the difficult-to-place W196 streamliner on under-developed Continental racing tyres thumps the course markers. Juan can only finish fourth.

On the grid at Reims – Karl Kling (left), Fangio, Marimón, and Prince 'Bira' before the start.

German GP 1954. Fangio and González on hearing of Marimón's death.

July 30, 1954 – Practice for the German GP, Nürburgring. Juan insisted upon an open-wheeled replacement for the 'Stromlinienwagen' W196 body on this demanding road circuit. He won, but 'Pinocho' Marimón had died in practice.

He insisted on a new open-wheeled version for the next round, the German Grand Prix. That was an important race for me. Mercedes' racing manager, Alfred Neubauer, had recommended that I should 'prove myself in a car of modern type' before I could be seriously considered as a potential works team driver. We had therefore bought a brand-new Maserati 250F, and by the time of the German GP, having lost Juan's services, Maserati considered I was doing a good enough job in my private car to receive works backing for the rest of the season.

For Fangio it was a tragic race, even though he won. He explains: 'In practice Moss had set excellent times in his private Maserati and this upset 'Pinocho' Marimón who was the number one factory team driver. On the Friday night I told him to stay calm and I would lead him round for one or two laps next day. But on that Saturday he did not wait, he went out on his own and crashed above Adenau Bridge and was killed.

'It was very difficult to drive afterwards, but that was our profession. It was a very, very sad day.'

González set off furiously to lead the race but Fangio passed him in the dipping high-speed flick beneath the Antoniusbuche Bridge at the end of the straight – one of the most dauntingly difficult swerves on the entire course. He then settled into a comfortable rhythm until Karl Kling stormed by in his sister Mercedes, driving really hard despite pit signals to steady down. Fangio was always very good at understanding another driver's keenness to excel in his home Grand Prix but he admits 'I was not very pleased when Kling passed me. Neubauer was going frantic in the pits, expecting us to break both cars, but every time I passed the pits I just pointed forward at Kling – he was the one setting the pace. Then something went wrong with his car's

suspension and the race was mine . . . But that was a very unhappy weekend.'

He won again in the Swiss GP, during wet practice for which I set fastest time of the session in my private, now works-supported Maserati. This really confirmed my promise in Neubauer's eyes and he apparently began to think of me for their '55 team as a team-mate to Fangio, who at Berne won again and sewed up his second World Championship title.

On 11 September Juan shared a Lancia sports car with Piero Taruffi in the Tourist Trophy at Dundrod and finished fourth, then to Monza for the Italian Grand Prix. There I managed to put my Maserati on the front row, beside Ascari's Ferrari and Fangio's inevitable Mercedes streamliner on pole.

In the race, Juan's car used up its brakes after ten laps so he couldn't keep up with my Maserati and Ascari's Ferrari. I managed to slingshot past them both into the Curva Grande, Ascari's engine broke soon after, and Juan slid off the track twice at the Porfido Curves. Near the end I was signalled to slow down and he was in such trouble that even then he couldn't close up. Twelve laps from the finish my car began to blow out oil, I stopped to add more but it ran straight out onto the track and my engine finally seized at the Porfido Curves. I pushed the car up to the line, Neubauer patting me on the shoulder as I panted by, and I sat on its tail waiting for Juan to win, before pushing across to be classified tenth. Being the great sportsman he is, Juan greeted me as the moral victor, and Pirelli even paid me a winner's bonus. I was bitterly disappointed, but at the same time elated, and Juan told everybody that I had at last 'arrived', which meant the world to me.

That was Juan's fourth GP victory of the season in

September 19, 1954 – Berlin GP, AVUS.

the silver cars. By that time his second World Championship title was already won, and yet again it had been totally his year.

At AVUS for the Berlin Grand Prix, Mercedes ran the streamliners again. 'Neubauer didn't actually tell us to finish in any particular order, but the management did generally drop hints and it was only fair that Kling should win in front of his home crowd. It was his country, his crowd and it was a German car, and so we crossed the line in formation, Kling ahead of me with Herrmann third.'

The last race of that season was the Spanish Grand Prix at Barcelona where Mercedes tried both streamlined and open-wheeled cars in practice before deciding to race the open-wheelers. Their straight-eight engine was fuel injected and demanded careful adjustment to atmospheric

conditions. For final practice, the weather was cool and overcast and the fuel injection was adjusted to run slightly more lean than might be normal at Barcelona. Raceday was then very hot and that injection setting proved too lean so the pistons burned. The cars also overheated after litter accumulated in their nose intakes. Fangio was soaked in hot oil and suffered some painful scalds. That was not my weekend – I had shunted the works 250F in practice and my own car packed up in the race.

But a few weeks later Neubauer invited me to join Mercedes as Juan's number two for the coming year and as he once again returned triumphantly to Buenos Aires and Balcarce as Champion of the World, I prepared to join him there early in the new year, eager to learn at the feet of the master – and maybe beat him.

*Daimler-Benz Museum,
Stuttgart-Unterturkheim, 1990.
1939 W154/163 as used by Fangio
in the Argentine, 1951*

*October 24, 1954 – Spanish GP,
Barcelona. Displaced World
Champion Alberto Ascari
congratulates his successor.*

*Daimler-Benz Museum W196s with
the 3-litre 300SLR engines for
Formule Libre racing, now used for
historic demonstrations, on
Mercedes' famous high-speed test
track at Unterturkheim, 1990.*

1955: Team-mates

During the new season, Mercedes-Benz extended its racing programme to include both the Formula 1 and Sports Car World Championship series, using the formidable new 300SLR sports-racing car developed from their F1 design.

The Argentine Grand Prix on 16 January was to be not only my début for Mercedes-Benz, but also my first visit to Juan's home country. It was run in 36°C in the shade – 51°C on the track! Juan admits: 'It was terribly hot, and very demanding. The heavy Mercedes was never a light car to handle, especially on the winding sections of the Autodrome and in that heat. Froilán and Ascari both went by but then Ascari spun off in the new Lancia D50 and Froilán began to suffer badly from the heat.

'Once I had established a lead I was determined to keep going. I felt there was great responsibility on me to do well for Mercedes. I was one of their dealers, they had just set up a factory in Argentina, they ran this great team and it was important to show them in their best light.

'After 35 laps the red petrol reserve light came on, so I stopped to refuel and rejoined third. I overtook Schell and Mieres and then it was just a matter of hanging on. To take my mind off the heat, which was so bad my right leg was being burned by a chassis tube heated by the exhaust, I made myself think of freezing mountain air, and told myself I was in waist-deep snow. I had to keep going, that snow was deep and freezing cold. That worked.'

He won, but he had to be helped from his car at the finish, and the doctors laid him on the pits floor and gave him fluids. Earlier, when my own engine had cut out due to a vapour lock somewhere in the overheated injection system, I was feeling groggy, but not half as groggy as the willing medics seemed to think, only freeing me from the ambulance into which I'd been bundled when an interpreter

was finally found. I took over Hans Herrmann's car and we finished fourth. But Juan had kept going implacably throughout, and he was 18 years older than me!

Two weeks later, he won the City GP, driving a W196 using the new 300SLR sports-car engine. Farina's Ferrari won the first Heat using Pirelli tyres which gave him more grip than our specially hard and long-wearing Continentals, but in Heat Two he spun and gave us a clear lap's lead. I passed Fangio to win by seconds, but he beat me overall on aggregate.

Back in Europe, Mercedes prepared for the Mille Miglia – opening round of the Sports Car Championship – as no team ever before, or since. Juan did two complete practice runs. He was intending to take with him his old Alfa Romeo mechanic Giulio Sala but Sala couldn't stand the buffeting of the twin-headrest two-man cockpit. So Juan decided to run solo instead. Sala was very disappointed, but Juan explains: 'After Urrutia's death, which I counted as my fault, I always preferred to drive alone, even in such a long race as the Mille Miglia.

'During the race I was heading down the old straight on the Pescara circuit, towards the control in Pescara itself, when Hans Herrmann caught me in his two-man 300SLR which he was sharing with Hermann Eger. It went past like an aeroplane. I tried really hard to keep up, but my car just would not go. Just beyond the control there was a Mercedes service depot and I told them "There's something wrong with the engine." They said "No, no, it's all right," and waved me away. The same happened at Rome.'

'At the Florence control I was not going to be told it's all right when I knew it was not. This time the mechanics had a really good look and they found that the rear injector pipe on top of the engine had been broken off

January 16, 1955 – Argentine GP, Buenos Aires. Juan repaying the debt he felt he owed Mercedes, thinking of cool, deep snow and ignoring the exhaust-heated chassis tube burning his leg – he raced on and on for 3hrs 00mins 38.6secs to win his second home Formula 1 GP.

by vibration, just above the pump. They changed the pipe but didn't think to fit a fresh spark plug. They waved me away again and I drove off, only to find it was still firing on only seven due to that dirty plug. We could not then change the plug before the finish in Brescia. It says quite a lot for the strength of those engines that mine misfired on seven cylinders at racing speed for almost a thousand miles without suffering serious damage.'

I won that race at record speed in the sister 300SLR while Juan finished fourth. But he played quite a role in my success as explained here.

Reunion – Fangio, Moss, Kling, Unterturkheim, 1990.

May Day, 1955 – Mille Miglia, Italy. Juan at speed in pursuit of Moss/Jenkinson's sister car in his 'seven-cylinder' Mercedes 300SLR.

THE MYSTERY OF FANGIO'S MAGIC PILLS

Juan's stamina in roasting heat became legendary amongst fellow drivers. He was blessed with a naturally very slow heart-rate and as a man who had worked physically hard all his life he was also tremendously fit.

He had built up remarkable physical endurance during his early career in ultra-long distance Carretera racing, but he also had some medical assistance, and when we were teamed together for Mercedes he offered me some little pills which he said would combat fatigue. I took one of these before my subsequent drive in the Mille Miglia, and won that race at record speed. Soon after the finish I drove overnight to Stuttgart for breakfast with the Daimler-Benz board, and then set off to the Channel ferry port and eventually drove all the way home – without sleeping. I wrote in my diary 'Fangio's pills are fantastic!'.

My father took an unused pill for chemical analysis, and the report said that it included some strange unidentifiable ingredient. The legend evolved that Fangio's magic pills must be some weird South American brew, made by a witch-doctor ... I wasn't conscious of knowing anything

about their true origin until we sat down during preparation of this book. Then we asked if they really had been some strange concoction from the Andes?

Juan just laughed. He thought that was a huge joke. 'No!' he said. 'Not at all. One day I told my doctor that the worst thing I always suffered in a long race was great thirst and he prescribed those pills. They were not South American, they were Swiss things, called 'Dynavis', and I was never troubled greatly by thirst ever again.'

Strangely enough, after hearing all this, I was looking for something else in my 1955 diary, and I found a cryptic and long forgotten note, reading simply 'Dynavis' – the trade name of those little pills – and 'Vister' – which I believe is the name of the company which made them.

We had cracked the mystery at the time, Juan must have explained but there were other more important things to think about and memory had long since buried it.

The '55 Mille Miglia was the only occasion on which I took one of those things, and perhaps – in that innocent age – none of us thought any more of it ...

The Monaco Grand Prix was back in the calendar that year, and Mercedes produced two short-wheelbase outboard front brake 'specials' for Fangio and me. During practice poor Hans Herrmann crashed and broke his leg. I set the fastest time, then Juan went out and bettered it. I lowered his new time, and he bettered it again. It was fun to be measuring myself against the undisputed master in a sister car, but it could be a little demoralizing. However hard you tried the Old Man always seemed to have a faster time in his back pocket!

In that race the unthinkable happened and both our Mercedes broke. Ascari crashed his Lancia into the harbour and fortunately swam to safety with nothing worse than a broken nose. It was an awful shock when he was killed at Monza the following Wednesday.

Lancia was devastated by his death which coincided savagely with their financial collapse. At Spa for the Belgian GP, Castellotti ran a lone Lancia D50 as a private entry. It was the only car we felt could match ours for pace, if not for reliability.

At Spa in practice, Castellotti beat Fangio's 1954 practice record by four seconds. Juan and I lined up alongside him and Eugenio Castellotti led from me with Fangio on my tail until he passed us both on the Masta Straight. It was fantastic experience, following him on such a very fast course, watching his line, watching his car's broad, silver tail swooping left and right from verge to verge, weaving around the hills, way above 160mph. Neubauer gave us a stiff talking-to about following so closely, because he foresaw us colliding.

The Eifelrennen non-Championship sports car race followed at Nürburgring. Juan won, with me second, right behind him. That was the only time he beat me in the

May 22, 1955 – Grand Prix d'Europe, Monte Carlo. Juan shows off his latest-model short-wheelbase Mercedes W196's new outboard front brakes. He much preferred this version to the older long-wheelbase inboard front-brake design.

Mercedes sports cars. I was very happy to run him as close as I did in the Grand Prix cars, but I always felt I had the edge in sports cars. Juan doesn't necessarily agree, but I like to think the record speaks for itself.

At Le Mans of course, he and I were teamed together and the SLRs became involved in the dreadful accident which wrecked that race. It was a terrible disaster and an awful sight, with over 80 killed and a hundred-plus injured; but Juan's luck – he says – preserved him, as he was right behind 'Levegh' ready to lap him, when the accident began.

He says, 'What I saw as we approached the pits after about two hours' racing, ready for the first pit stops, was Hawthorn's Jaguar overtaking Macklin's Austin-Healey on the left and then his brake lights going on as he pulled across to the right to stop at his pits for the first refuelling. Macklin then had to dodge to the left to pass the slowing Jaguar. 'Levegh' was just in front of me and I was about to lap him when Macklin moved into his path. I saw him throw up his hand as he moved across towards the left side bank, trying to squeeze through. He was doing maybe 125mph and me 135 and he just ran straight up the sloping tail of the British car and crashed onto the top of the left-side bank and the engine and front end of his car broke away and went through the crowd.

'I saw Macklin's car bouncing off the pit-wall on the right and in a split-second I was through and it was all behind me. I could not believe how I had got through because the gap had been closing so rapidly I was sure no way would my car fit. Yet somehow it had. I had felt no impact at all, yet in the pits afterwards there were dents and green paint on my car, which could only have come from Macklin's, or bits of it.

'On my next lap down the straight past Hunaudiéres

I looked across the inside of the circuit and could see the smoke. I began to shake. But even then I had no real idea of the magnitude of the disaster when I was signalled in to hand over to Moss.'

We were leading that night when the order came from Stuttgart to withdraw in respect. Mercedes was a German team racing in France only ten years after the wartime occupation, but I could see no sense in withdrawing and I told them so. It proved nothing and handed Jaguar victory on a plate. Juan felt happier at withdrawing than I – but he had been on the spot when the accident began, which I had not.

After that catastrophe, four Championship GPs were cancelled. The Dutch went ahead and Juan and I finished 1-2 in what the press called 'The Train'.

The British Grand Prix was at Aintree. I don't know to this day whether Juan let me win or not. I've never really thought it fair to ask him – though he admits that Mercedes' public relations director might have hinted that I should win. I'd like to think I won it fair and square but I'm just not sure. In any case that was my first win in a Championship-qualifying Grand Prix.

We took the SLRs to the Swedish Grand Prix at Kristianstad, which was the only place where Neubauer ever issued a finishing order, telling me I should place second while Fangio should win – which we did.

At Monza for the Italian Grand Prix, which was to be Mercedes' last Formula 1 race, Piero Taruffi was in the team and he really wanted to win on his home circuit. On the last lap only he and Fangio were left of our team and leaving the first banked curve Juan saw him closing fast in his mirrors. 'I watched him carefully, and we finished in formation with me winning by 0.7 second...' Juan was

July 16, 1955 – British GP, Aintree. Moss's magic Mercedes moment leading Fangio across the finish line by 0.2 sec to win his first World Championship-qualifying Grand Prix.

A poster for the 1955 German Grand Prix which was cancelled in the wake of the Le Mans disaster.

June 11, 1955 – Le Mans 24-Hours. Saturday afternoon's fantastic initial two-hour 'Grand Prix' raged between Mike Hawthorn's works Jaguar D-Type and Juan Manuel Fangio's factory Mercedes-Benz 300SLR – until the first pit-stops, and disaster. The Jaguars used their disc brakes to the full, the Mercedes' drums being augmented by the airbrake flap seen raised on Juan's car here in the Esses.

115

September 11, 1955 – Italian GP,
Monza. The sport's first three-time
World Champion Driver.

October 16, 1955 – Targa Florio,
Sicily. A long delay in the pits with
a jammed oil filler flap prevented
Fangio and Kling in this 300SLR
pushing Moss and Collins harder in
their's. Juan was never very
fortunate in sports cars.

World Champion driver again – for the third time – and I was second on points in his slipstream. After that it was back to the SLRs. Juan remembers: 'At the Dundrod TT Hawthorn and I raced again just as in the opening stages at Le Mans, my Mercedes against his Jaguar, but Moss drove brilliantly that day to win.' Juan finished fourth.

Championship points earned there gave Mercedes the chance of pipping Ferrari to the Sports Car Championship if they could beat them in the Targa Florio in Sicily. The effort they mounted there was similar to that for the Mille Miglia. Peter Collins co-drove an SLR with me, while Juan teamed-up with his usual partner, Karl Kling. Peter and I had a torrid race, ending up with a very battered but winning car, while Fangio/Kling lost a lot of time in the pits with their car's oil filler cap jammed shut, but eventually finished second. Mercedes had clinched the double Championship titles which they had aimed at.

Juan had wanted to return to South America as a worthy World Champion and Maserati provided a 300S sports car for him to drive on 6 November in the Gran Premio Venezuela at Caracas. For him it was possibly his most difficult race that year. The strong Ferrari team was running very powerful cars. It was terribly hot, it was a long 85-lap race and very tiring. Juan recalls: 'My water temperature looked high but the mechanics assured me it was just the gauge over-reading. As a precaution I chose not to believe them and treated the gauge as accurate, varying my speed to keep the temperature stable. I was leading until I half-spun and then had to hold off de Portago. Towards the end it clouded over, and in the cooler conditions I could force harder and broke the lap record, built a good lead and won. I had wanted to show well on that return to South America, and my luck helped it work out for me – again.'

Prof Dr Fritz Nallinger, Chief Engineer of Daimler-Benz AG, presents Juan with his diamond set three-pointed star to honour his role in the team's double-World Championship win.

The collection of Mercedes three-pointed star gold and diamond 'pins' – awarded to Fangio.

TRICKS OF THE TRADE

I was always fascinated by the manner in which Juan went about his work. He had a cool and logical approach which normally involved winning at the lowest possible speed, and he would set his rhythm, and his pace, to offset the pressure being applied by the guy in second place. 'To finish first, you must first finish . . .' One cannot argue with that perfect logic, but I always took a different, instinctive view. I liked to have a dice, a real old tear-up and to me that was the name of the game.

Juan always looked a little bit tubby but boy was he fit! 'During my International career, when I returned to race in Argentina each January the temperatures there were fantastically high. So each year when I got home I would go and play football on the beach for three or four hours with the local lads through the height of the midday sun. I would do this every day for 15 days in succession after arriving from Europe. That was my training. The rest of the time simply driving the cars of our time kept us fit!

'I always had to watch my diet carefully and my routine on race day was to have a very light meal around 11 in the morning before the race which usually started around 3 in the afternoon. And then after a little wine I would rest. I would go to bed and think about the race and turn over in my mind the possible developments and possible ways to handle whatever might arise. I would just quietly consider the best way to deal with it.

'On the night before a race I always liked to drive around the circuit for three or four final laps, using the headlights in the dark, just to fix in my mind every feature of the course. This was so that should anything unusual happen next day I would know exactly where there was an extra piece of concrete, or where I could perhaps cut one corner to get a better line through the next . . .

'It was also very important to do the fastest lap for pole position because that would enable you to discover the limit of the car and of yourself on the particular course that weekend. This was the key to success, for you could try and check things in practice, while in the race you could not experiment in any way. So, by the time the race began I knew exactly how late I could possibly brake into any corner and where I dare not and how hard to accelerate and in what gear.

'Whenever I was given a fresh car I would ask the mechanics, where is the maximum torque of the engine, at what revs? Then I would drive precisely to those revs and change up around that point to have the engine's maximum torque working constantly. There was no point in revving higher towards the red line: the power would only fall away and you would be risking the life of the engine.

'During the race itself I would settle into a rhythm and try always to do everything exactly the same, to repeat the pattern, on every lap. I used to think "I can reach maximum revs at that tree", and then next time I would think "I have to reach maximum revs at that tree", and again, and again — every lap. Once the pattern is established, it's very easy. In just the same way, it is equally important to know your maximum limits in life too . . .'

Following Juan closely — as I did so often in the Mercedes — I could watch that pattern at close quarters, and most of the time at very high speed. His precision was fantastic: he never went off the road but he would run constantly right to its very edge. He would do that lap after lap and just keep up that same intense pressure — all of the time. Try as hard as I might, the distance between us didn't really change very much. Normally, following someone close is a frustrating business, but following Fangio was not

at all frustrating: the thrill of being able to live with the man at those heights of performance was deeply enjoyable. Sometimes he would tweak his car sideways in a corner and I'd run up inside him and then I would pull a face at him and he would grin back and we would go hell for leather into the next corner. I tell you, it was fun ...

Fangio was also a tremendously intelligent driver. He was always terrific through traffic, he had great vision, and superb tactical forethought. And he could keep his times up all day long. His driving pattern was flat, not up and down, and other drivers could not do that.

How Fangio went through the crash at Le Mans unscathed reveals an amazing extra sense which the very best drivers each had. That extra sense showed itself in a different way at Albi in '53 when the brakes failed in his BRM. Juan ascribes that to his luck, but I believe you can make your own good luck, or at least assist it a little ... I believe in that incident at Le Mans, Juan got through by thinking that much faster than perhaps his conscious reflexes told him he was capable of doing. He took his decision, perhaps almost before he realized he had made it, and it was the right decision. That is making your own luck.

Practice was always far more dangerous than the race. More mechanical failures occurred in practice, and oil on the circuit was very possible then.

When Juan and I shared a sports car drive together, as at Le Mans for Mercedes or in Buenos Aires or Nürburgring for Maserati, the engineers would ask. 'How would you like the car set up?' – 'Whatever Moss is having ...' We would compromise to the extent that I would use his wider seat, but otherwise the technical set-up was normally mine with Juan cheerfully accepting it.

Describing his driving technique, Juan still maintains a cheerful veil over some finer points, but I think he enjoys our interest. He describes how 'When I entered a curve very fast I would touch the brake lightly with my heel just to settle the car and only then press the brakes with the full foot. The vital thing was to keep the car settled and balanced under braking, and then to maintain similar balance in a different manner under acceleration. This balance and the consistent pattern you establish is the key.'

Ask him what his favourite circuits were and he beams at the memories: 'I liked the fastest circuits, like Spa, magnificent! And the Nürburgring too for different reasons because it was so varied and such an enormous challenge. A circuit that was a bit dangerous was good for me, because there you could tell the difference between us all, and my luck never really let me down ...

'I had not a single fright in all my racing that ever stayed with me. I have had too much from life and I don't regret a single thing.'

August 5, 1956 – German GP, Nürburgring. Juan on pole position in the Lancia-Ferrari D50A, flanked by his team-mates Collins and Castellotti with Moss's Maserati on the outside of the row. Juan's spare goggles are protected inside the collar of his sports-shirt.

1956: The Hardest Year

After clinching both the World Championships in 1955, Mercedes-Benz withdrew from motor racing to concentrate on developing production models. It was sad both for Fangio and for me, because the German team had been the greatest in so many ways. But both of us were in demand. I eventually signed up with Maserati, for whom I had last driven on a works-supported basis in 1954, while Fangio finally joined Ferrari after an exceedingly difficult off-season.

'When Mercedes-Benz retired I thought of retiring as well. I had had a very good international career since 1949 and had won the World Championship more times than anybody else. After the Targa Florio, Enzo Ferrari phoned and asked me to see him with a view to driving for his team in 1956. He said "I know you cost a lot, but I need you."

'He did not need me badly enough to agree terms at that meeting... I then went to drive for Maserati in Caracas, but difficult things were developing at home.'

On 16 September 1955 Perón had been toppled in Argentina, and the new régime set up an investigative body to examine the affairs of personalities linked with the Peronist period. This list included Juan.

He was in Caracas, preparing to drive the Maserati 300S in the GP there, when friends from Buenos Aires telephoned to warn him of this new decree and advised him not to return home. He was made of sterner stuff. He told them 'I've got nothing to hide from any investigation,' and insisted he was coming home, no matter what. That was typical of the man, because one should never confuse his humility, gentleness and good manners with weakness. He has always been an enormously strong and courageous man – both physically and ethically.

He won at Caracas for Maserati, but there was an unhappy dispute over whether he or the company should keep the trophy. In the end they presented it to him, but as a result of the argument he resumed negotiations with Ferrari, using as an intermediary an Italian journalist-cum-racing-entrepreneur named Marcello Giambertone. *Dona* Andreina, Fangio's girlfriend and constant companion during this period – we all thought she was his wife but in fact they never married – liked Giambertone and so he was taken on and began to portray himself as Fangio's manager, which wasn't totally accurate.

Subsequently, Giambertone wrote what purported to be Juan's autobiography, *My Twenty Years of Racing*. It included a highly critical chapter about Ferrari, and Mr Ferrari in particular. This caused quite a rift between these two motor racing giants, which was only finally bridged in 1987 at the celebrations to commemorate the Ferrari marque's fortieth anniversary. Juan has always avoided controversy, and the words published had certainly not been written by him. He pointedly disowns them.

After Caracas he returned home, and on his way through Peru he visited Huanchasco, kneeling deep in thought at the little memorial where Urrutia had died.

He then flew to Buenos Aires. 'That was a very unpleasant homecoming. The Government put three inspectors onto me. The first two were corrupt, but finally we got a decent Inspector, a capable man who became a friend. He then worked with us through that *interdicción* for four years until I was completely cleared. I had been the figurehead of a racing programme supported enthusiastically by Perón but I never had any direct political involvement. I was a proud Argentine and I drove proudly for myself, for Balcarce, for my friends and for Argentina.

'People on the *interdicción* list were forbidden to

July 14, 1956 – British GP Silverstone. Fangio, Lancia-Ferrari, fighting his pain.

leave the country, so I had to see the Minister for Foreign Affairs to ask permission. I explained I had an invitation to race abroad; if I was forbidden I would have to tell the team in question the real reason I could not accept. He said there was no problem, I could go – so I joined Ferrari.'

He began that difficult year in the V8 Lancia-Ferraris in the Argentine Gran Premio on 22 January. During the race his fuel pump failed, was repaired in a pit-stop but then failed again. He waited for Musso to be called in and then took over his car, rejoining a lap behind the leader – me.

On his fourth lap in Musso's car he slithered off and got stuck in mud from earlier rain. A friend named Fortunato Firpo who was acting as a track marshal, and the Uruguayan driver Bayardo, pushed him out. 'I expected to be black-flagged but nothing happened so I pressed on. Ferrari fitted a very low first gear intended to be used only for starting. Coming through the ess-bend on one lap I tried this gear instead of second and it catapulted me out much faster. After that I used it every lap. I caught and passed Mendítéguy, and I broke my Mercedes lap record by nearly

three seconds. Then I caught Moss.'

He passed my Maserati on lap 80 as my engine was roughening up. We used to run exotic methanol fuel brews in those days and in the heat at Buenos Aires Maserati's fuel-mixers had been a little too ambitious! Two laps after Juan passed me my engine broke. Our team manager at Maserati protested that Juan had received illegal outside assistance, but the protest and subsequent appeal were both rejected, and Juan shared his win with Musso.

He and Castellotti then retired a Ferrari 860 Monza sports in the 1,000kms and at Mendoza he won the City GP yet again. Then he and Castellotti won the Sebring 12-Hours handsomely – his first-ever win in the USA.

The first race in Europe was the Syracuse GP, which Juan won again. So he'd driven five times for his new team and won four times. Word was that he needed the money! He was certainly earning it. He was as skilled and fast and virtually unbeatable as ever.

For the Mille Miglia he drove a big Ferrari 290MM, and finished fourth after a truly epic drive – even by his standards. It is today remarkably little recognised.

THE HARDEST RACE – 1956 MILLE MIGLIA

For the '56 Mille Miglia, I and my navigator from 1955 – Denis Jenkinson of Motor Sport *– were out to win for the second year running, this time in a Maserati. But the under-developed 3.5-litre car we were given proved to be a real rolling disaster. It was a poorly-balanced, hastily prepared and barely finished lash-up which was undeniably fast but which understeered really badly.*

Heavy rain poured down on race day and eventually I lost the Maserati comprehensively. Jenks and I crashed through a roadside barrier high up in the hills and all that saved us from somersaulting maybe 300 feet down the mountainside into a rock-strewn stream was a rather puny little tree. Fortunately it was big enough to stop us. We had just scrambled out, persuaded each other we were still alive, and clambered back up to road level when we heard the deep roar of an approaching Ferrari. It was Fangio, and he came splashing round towards us, recognized Jenks and me and stopped – remember this is slap in the middle of the great Mille Miglia – to ask if we were OK!

He said he'd try to get help sent back out to us, and then Jenks reminded him that this was a motor race and he ought to be racing and he just pulled a face, blew a stream of water off the end of his nose, and drove away.

If that race had been uncomfortable for us, at least it was shorter than the race which he endured:

'Listen, I tell you that was the worst race I ever drove in. It was complete torture.' Fangio told me later.

'The night before the start, when they filled the car with fuel, they found the tank was leaking. It was late, and rather than remove the tank to seal the leak they removed a rear wheel and cut a hole in the body to get at it. This hole
was just behind the cockpit. They mended the tank and put it all back together, but they forgot to re-seal the hole in the bodywork.

'Next day it rained and rained. The wheel was spraying water from the road straight into the cockpit. Water was being pumped in faster than it could run out through all the little gaps and holes there are in such a car. At the Ravenna depot I asked the mechanics to cut a hole in the floor to let the water drain away. They did that quickly and I drove off again into the storm, but all that happened then was that the water came up straight through the drain hole they had just cut and the cockpit filled even faster!

'At high speed the water was spraying up like a fountain over my chest and under my visor. Near Modena I stopped at a restaurant called La Parola where they knew me because I used to stop there when passing by. They gave me a brandy and a leather coat which I was very grateful to put on for extra warmth and protection and I climbed back in and got going again.

'The water affected the ignition and the engine began to misfire but I didn't want to give up because that would mean being stranded miles from anywhere, and well – it was the Mille Miglia . . .

'Towards the finish my hands were frozen stiff: I could neither unclench my fingers nor grasp the wheel and gearshift properly. I was numb right through and shivering. At Brescia, when I finished fourth, I was so relieved. All I wanted was a hot deep bath. I lay in it, and my lips swelled right up, an extraordinary reaction to the beating my face had taken in the rain, and perhaps the brandy too? That was very uncomfortable – a little frightening. I had really abused my body that day. It was my hardest race.'

March 25, 1956 – Sebring 12-hours, Florida. Juan's first win in the USA made his name big news. He shared the works Ferrari Monza 860 with Eugenio Castellotti (right) yet another of his younger team-mates who both revered him and revelled in the privilege of driving with him.

Fangio retired from the International Trophy at Silverstone and then on 13 May the World Championship recommenced with the Monaco Grand Prix. He finished second, in Peter Collins's car, but it had been another very hard race for him.

I led the opening lap in my Maserati with Juan on my tail but as I accelerated out of Ste Devote I just glimpsed him – astonishingly – sideways in my mirrors as he spun on oil. His car struck the retaining wall, displacing its de Dion axle. He got going again but the car was handling like a pig, jinking to one side under braking and to the other under acceleration. Aiming to pass cars must have been like trying to shoot clay pigeons with someone nudging your elbow. Even so, he barrelled back past Behra, Collins and Castellotti to regain second place behind me. Then his clutch began to hang up; he missed a gear at the Tabac, ran wide

and clouted the wall. He pulled into the pits and Collins was brought in on lap 54 to hand over his car. Juan rejoined third, 49 seconds behind me. He caught Behra and with 20 laps to go was 39 secs behind. I knew I could give him two seconds a lap and still be ahead at the finish, so I paced those final stages and eventually beat him by 6.1 seconds.

It was my second win in a Grande Épreuve, the first of my three wins at Monaco and the first time I had beaten Juan in another team's Grand Prix car. As always he was wonderful in defeat. He just seemed pleased for me.

At the Nürburgring 1,000kms he finished second with Castellotti in a Monza 860 – while I won again for Maserati, sharing with Taruffi, Schell and Jean Behra. I also shared the 3rd and 4th placed cars! Then at Spa for the Belgian GP the Lancia-Ferrari was in its element, as Juan

*1956 German GP – No hard words
in the Ferrari pit. Fangio and Peter
Collins actually got on famously,
the young Englishman playing very
much the pupil role. His
sportsmanship in surrendering his
own World Championship chance
at Monza for Juan to take his fourth
title was unforgettable.*

recalls: 'I was given a very fast car for that race but I couldn't get good times in practice until I tried the muletto and went more quickly. I seemed particularly well supported by the seat in that car, it gripped me around the back and shoulders as well as at my legs. I had it mounted in my original car and immediately gained two seconds a lap! I kept that particular seat for the rest of the season.'

In the race Juan was in a commanding lead until his diff seized – out of oil. Pete Collins was left to win, and I was third after setting fastest lap.

Fangio and Castellotti were third in the Supercortemaggiore sports car race at Monza in a Ferrari 500 Testa Rossa and then on 1 July came Reims and the French Grand Prix. 'That was a bad race for me because the car let me down again in a silly way when I thought I was going to win. Collins and Castellotti and I were running in formation when Schell caught us up in the Vanwall which was very fast indeed on the long straights. At first we thought he was a lap behind but he had been going so fast after an early delay he had caught us up and was on the same lap. When we appreciated that, we really began racing, but then I felt a cool spray and smelled fuel and realized I was being showered by fuel forced from the back of the pressure gauge.

'That was a nasty moment – all it needed was a spark or exhaust blow-back and finito! I would have been roasted alive. We raced until Schell's Vanwall broke. I was drenched with fuel and stopped at the pits where they fixed the pipe but my chance of winning was gone. I was still soaked in fuel, and I finished fourth while Peter Collins won again.

'Castellotti was very upset after that race. I went over to him to shake hands thinking he had just won at last but he said "I'm so angry, they made me slow down to team orders. I don't want to race any more if that's the way we have to play it." I always liked Castellotti – he was a nice lad – and to show solidarity I said "Castellotti, I'm with you. If Castellotti doesn't race for Ferrari any more, Fangio doesn't race for Ferrari any more either."

'Then I saw that Castellotti had gone to race for Ferrari at Rouen, regardless of what he had said in hot blood at Reims. I was very embarrassed and told Giambertone to explain all this to Ferrari, saying "It's best that you leave me free." But Mr Ferrari came back to me and said "We need you," so I said "OK, but I want an exclusive mechanic dedicated to my car," and they gave him to me. I could not risk a repetition of the bad preparation shown at Spa or specially Reims – they could have burned me to a crisp. After also being nearly drowned and frozen in the Mille Miglia I don't think I was being unreasonable.

'I had been quite badly burned – chemical burns – by the fuel soaked into my clothes and I developed what Italians call "St Antonio's Fire" – a most painful condition. I swelled up all red and raw around my middle. At the pre-race medical at Silverstone the English doctor was shocked by the sight and said "You're not fit – you can't race." I told him "OK, you tell your race organisers and sort it out with them." I was allowed to race.

'Our Englebert tyres were very hard indeed and I came back through the race when the others began to wear their tyres and started sliding about. Moss was leading in the Maserati 250F but then he retired and left me to win. I had won by my luck again – and by the pain-killing tablets prescribed by the doctors. I felt so bad immediately after that race that I actually fainted, even before I had time to have my usual post-race bath – I just went out like a light, zonk! That was the only race I ever won in England.'

The Lancia-Ferrari understeered round Silverstone, but Juan found it very good at the Nürburgring for the German Grand Prix. 'It was much more nimble and better-braked than the Mercedes of '54. My only real rivals were my team-mates. Collins was challenging for fastest lap and I had to lower my practice time by ten seconds to beat him. He pushed too hard and had to retire at the pits, and took over de Portago's car but didn't last long. Halfway through the race my Ferrari was alone and I just concentrated upon keeping it all together until the finish.'

Guess who was second? That's right, me in the Maserati, but I just couldn't get close to the Old Boy that day, although we traded fastest lap back and forth.

The Italian Grand Prix at Monza would decide the World Championship. Peter Collins was the only driver who could deny Juan his fourth World title, and his third in a row.

'Our team was 1-2-3 in practice but our cars had troubles with their Englebert tyres and I knew this could cost us the race. I suggested to my team-mates Castellotti and Musso that I should set the pace and that ten laps from the end I would pull over and let them fight it out to win the race as Italians, in Italian cars in Italy's most important race. Third or fourth place would still be good enough for me to win the Championship. But they said "No," they wanted to drive their own races.

'I took the lead and settled into my rhythm when sure enough they went rocketing by. They were driving too hard, abusing their tyres terribly. It was obvious they could not last. On the fourth lap they went in to change their tyres. Moss was leading for Maserati and Schell was very fast and pressing me in the Vanwall. But my car felt strange, and then under braking the right-front wheel veered out-

August 5, 1956 – German GP Nürburgring. Juan won this classical race three times and twice finished second in it. Here he is on the way to his second win, in the Lancia-Ferrari V8.

wards. I thought it must be loose. To check I jabbed the brake on the banking and the car flicked into a spin. I coasted into the pits with the wheel flapping loose: a drilled steering arm had snapped clean through!'

He spent 19 laps in the pits, resigned to having lost his World Championship hat-trick. De Portago was to hand over his car should Fangio hit trouble, but he had already retired. Musso was signalled to come in but ignored the signs. When he came in to change tyres he still refused to surrender his car, Juan believes quite rightly, in his home race. He was always hugely understanding.

'Then Collins came in to change his rear tyres and saw me stuck there and, without anyone asking him, he immediately offered me his car. That was a fantastic gesture. I hugged and kissed him and got into his car and finished second, and so I won the World Championship again, thanks to Collins and his English sense of sportsmanship.'

September 2, 1956 – Italian GP, Monza. Internecine warfare commences in the World Championship decider as Luigi Musso's Lancia-Ferrari blares into an immediate lead from the sister cars of Eugenio Castellotti and Fangio the eventual winner. Stirling Moss following in Maserati '36'. Juan's saviour, Peter Collins, has his Lancia-Ferrari '26' in a big wheel-spinning tailslide against the pit-lane.

Enzo Ferrari himself, during his annual practice visit to Monza at Italian GP time, lines up his star driver for Bernard Cahier to record the scene.

1957: Sheer Genius

For 1957, after much soul-searching, I finally decided I had found a worthy British Grand Prix car in the Vanwall. As I left my old friends and the chummy family atmosphere at Maserati, so Fangio returned there, the old rift forgotten. Because Vanwall built no sports cars, I stayed with Maserati for that series – so Juan and I became team-mates and rivals on alternate weekends.

Tony Vandervell, who ran the Vanwall team, had no interest in tackling the Argentine Grand Prix which opened the season – it would interrupt his company's development programme in preparation for the European rounds, and in any case Buenos Aires was simply too far away. Consequently, Maserati invited me to team up – if only temporarily – with Juan and Jean Behra and they fielded three new 'Lightweight' cars for us in the Buenos Aires Autodrome.

I set fastest time in practice but in the race my car's throttle linkage parted at the start and I lost nine laps having it repaired. I quite enjoyed the fight back. I recovered a lap on Juan and set fastest time – but could only finish eighth.

Meanwhile, up at the front of the field, Juan notched up yet another home victory after Jean Behra had led for some time. Juan had forgotten to close his engine's ventilation slats during the opening lap so it took a while to reach full operating temperature and consequently to develop full power. Later a damper broke, and ten laps from the finish they both had to refuel. 'But my mechanics got me going again more quickly and I won.'

We then shared Maserati's big new 450S V8 sports car – they called it the 'Bazooka' – in the Buenos Aires 1,000kms. It would top 180mph and accelerated from 0-100 in around 11 seconds. I handed over the lead to Juan

January 13, 1957 – Argentine GP, Buenos Aires. Wheeling out the latest 'Lightweight' Maserati 250 F at the 'Fangiodrome'.

Sebring '57

*January 13, 1957 – Argentine GP,
Buenos Aires. Juan's new works
Maserati leads Moss's, both fitted
with goose-neck cockpit ventilators
on the scuttle, Juan winning his
fourth consecutive home GP.*

March 23, 1957 – Sebring 12-Hours, Florida.

*March 23, 1957 – Sebring
12-Hours, Hendrick Field, Florida.
Juan stands back as co-driver Jean
Behra takes over their winning
Maserati 450S 'Bazooka' at a
scheduled pit-stop.*

after 33 laps and after 15 more he'd lapped everybody except Castellotti in Masten Gregory's Ferrari. Then our car's clutch failed and changing gear without it eventually broke the gearbox, which put us out.

In the Buenos Aires City GP, hot as ever at the Autodrome, Fangio won the 20-lap first Heat and finished third in the second, sufficient to win overall – yet again – on addition of times.

In Cuba, Juan won at Havana in a 300S and with Behra won Sebring in the big 450S. Then at Monaco on 19 May the World Championship recommenced and we were again racing against one another, my Vanwall versus his Lightweight Maserati. He promptly qualified on pole from Collins' Lancia-Ferrari and me.

'I had carburettor problems in that race,' Juan recalls, 'they flooded under acceleration and so straight from the start my car faltered and Moss got away. At Ste Dévote I let Collins go by to chase Moss. On the fourth lap Moss's brakes seemed to fail at the chicane and he crashed straight on, scattering telegraph poles from the barrier across the track. Collins crashed on the left, I found a clear gap to go through, (my luck again, you see), and Stirling's team-mate Tony Brooks – there was another very fine driver, I tell you – braked sharply. Behind him, Hawthorn was taken by surprise and his Ferrari rammed the Vanwall's tail, lost a wheel and ended-up over Collins' car on top of the barrier beside the harbour.

'So all the young English boys except Brooks were out and I was left alone in the lead. Brooks put tremendous pressure on me, but I just drove harder to break his heart. Finally he relaxed and settled for second.

'And I relaxed and settled for first.'

May 19, 1957 – Monaco GP, Monte Carlo.

Juan leading in the 'Lightweight' Maserati, passing the Hawthorn ('26') and Collins ('28') Lancia-Ferrari wrecks at the harbourside chicane.

The Monaco GP trophy presented by Prince Rainier and Princess Grace.

August 4, 1957 – German GP, Nürburgring. The day was Fangio's, in the 'Lightweight' 250F, seen here in the Karussel.

The Nürburgring 1,000kms followed – a hugely complicated race for Maserati. The 450S which Juan and I were sharing lost a wheel, so he joined Schell/Herrmann in a 300S which retired and then leapfrogged into the Godia/Gould 300S which then lay tenth. With Fangio driving, it finished fifth.

The Italian privateer Luigi Piotti then lent him his 300S to win the Portuguese GP, and then came Rouen where Fangio won the French Grand Prix in his Lightweight 250F.

In the Reims Grand Prix – a non-championship race that year – he retired. I played no part in either of those events. After Le Mans, which Juan never entered again due to his experience there in '55, I'd come a cropper while water-skiing at La Napoule, near Cannes, and developed a terrible sinus infection. I didn't race again until the British

GP at Aintree. There I was to drive nursing my sore hooter, while Tony Brooks my team-mate was nursing sore everything after rolling an Aston Martin at Le Mans.

But it was our day at Aintree, as Juan's Maserati let him down and in any case our Vanwalls were clearly superior. My first car struck trouble and Tony handed over his, which in his battered condition he was quite happy to do. We became the first Englishmen ever to win our home Grand Prix, and the first Brits to win a Grande Épreuve in a British car since Sir Henry Segrave had won the French GP at Tours for Sunbeam way back in 1923.

Again, Juan was one of the first to congratulate us.

So then off we went to Nürburgring, anticipating a rare old battle between the Vanwalls and Fangio in his Lightweight 250F on a circuit in which both of us delighted.

FANGIO'S GREATEST RACE

Juan explains the story of the incredible 1957 German Grand Prix like this: 'We expected the Vanwalls to be the strongest threat but the moment practice began they were in terrible trouble with suspension and road holding. The Ferraris then became our greatest challenge, and their hard Englebert tyres allowed them to run non-stop throughout the race. Our Pirellis were softer, so they wore quicker, but gave more grip and so we could lap faster. The mechanics did some trial runs and found they could refuel and change both rear wheels on our cars in 30 seconds. Bertocchi told me 'If you can build 30 seconds lead halfway through the race, we will change your tyres in 30 seconds.'

The track had been resurfaced and in practice Juan took pole 24.5 seconds inside his old Mercedes mark and 25.6 seconds inside the best Lancia-Ferrari time.

From the start, running light with half full tank against the brimming Lancia-Ferraris, Juan recalls how he 'just sat back to let Hawthorn and Collins lead. They were changing places which I thought was unnecessary, they were playing around. I kept behind for the first two laps and then on the third I overtook them both.

'By mid-race I had a 28 second lead, and on lap 12 I made my stop to refuel and fit fresh tyres. I got out, had a drink, Bertocchi and Ugolini told me the position but the mechanics were very slow. My 28 second lead vanished and then we lost another 48 seconds before I could get going again. I had been poised to win the race and my fifth World Championship there and I felt terribly disappointed. There were only ten laps left and I felt there was little chance of winning, unless I could do something special.

'First I had to bed in the new tyres so next lap I was 51 seconds behind the Ferraris. Although at that stage I knew Hawthorn was leading, I did not realise there were two of them still up there. I then began to use higher gears through the corners. This gave less precise control of the car's attitude when it was sliding, but as long as I entered the corners absolutely right, I knew I could reach higher revs along the following straight. There was a lack of grip in the higher gears but it was worth the risk for the time I could make up.

'The swerves through the dip beneath the bridge at the end of the main straight, where I had passed Froilán in 1954, offered a great time saving. I normally took it in fifth gear, just lifting off the throttle a little, trying to skim the crest rather than to jump over it so as not to upset the car on landing. In that race I did not lift my foot at all.

'I kept as far to the inside as I could and just let the car take off. It soared along and landed way across on the right of the track right up against the fence, and I could see the dust cloud I raised there when I glanced in my mirror. But I knew right then that I'd saved seconds, treating those two separate sections of straight absolutely as one. It was not something I would consider doing every lap of every race there, but that year was special.

'When I had first rejoined and initially lost more time, the Ferrari pit had signalled their drivers to relax. So while I was closing up on them, they were coming back a little towards me. Now I had made up 10 seconds and the pit had to wait another whole lap before signalling their drivers that I was closing up.

'I believe I was inspired that day. I never drove quite like that before, and I never drove quite like that ever again.

August 4, 1957 – German GP,
Nürburgring. 'That day I did things
I would never attempt again.'

'After 20 laps I saw a red speck far ahead and I
began telling myself "That is a Ferrari and it's leading the
race, you must win and you are going to catch it." The pits
had always signalled me one car, only one, I had not
realised there were two. On the Adenau descent I glimpsed
them both. Past the pits I was tailing them. Into the
penultimate lap along the straight behind the pits I got
inside Collins and overtook him but pressed too hard and
ran wide out of that curve. This let him repass me and move
across to the inside for the following corner. I stuck right
on his tail – keeping up the pressure – until we reached a
short straight up to a bridge. I moved up alongside him
there, and this time he gave way, and we then went down
into what we called the bob-run – the Fuchsröhre – into a
right-hand bend, and there was Hawthorn's leading Ferrari
right in front of me. I was working out where I could pass
him when after a series of curves came a short straight
ending in a 90-degree left, followed by an equally sharp
turn to the right. On the straight Hawthorn pulled to the
right to take his line so I shot up inside him. Hawthorn
suddenly pulled aside as if I had startled him, but I made a
point of pulling away before we reached the straight so he
could not slipstream me. Just in case he should try, I then
kept up that pressure for the whole lap – and so I won.

'Hawthorn and Collins were so good over their
defeat, they were so happy it seemed almost as if they had
beaten me. They were slapping me on the back and shaking
my hands even though Collins had his goggles smashed by
a stone thrown up from my car. They were both very good
lads, like Stirling too.'

136

June 1990 – Juan reunited with his 1957 German GP winner, now owned by Hartmut Ibing, in the same Nürburgring paddock garage which Maserati had used that year.

137

At Pescara, I beat Fangio, and my Vanwall was clearly superior to his Maserati down the long, long straight, and also handled pretty well through the twisty bits.

At Monza, Tony Brooks, Stuart Lewis-Evans and I qualified our three Vanwalls on the front row and they changed the grid formation to 4-3-4 to put a red car up there with us — inevitably it was Juan's Maserati, on the outside of the row. He recalls the race:

'At both Pescara and Monza the Vanwalls were faster on the straight. Their more sophisticated chassis and suspension and streamlined body shape also showed advantages round the corners. At Monza their negative camber at the rear wheels gave them much more grip around the Parabolica, where our cars' tails would slide out. Their four-cylinder engines also had very good initial acceleration at the start of the straights, and their shape made them very quick towards the end of them. I tried desperately hard in that race but there could be no miracle like at the Nürburgring — Moss still beat me.'

On the drive down to Modena for the non-Championship F1 GP in Maserati's and Ferrari's own backyard, Juan took an American ex-serviceman hitch-hiker along with him and *dona* Andreina in the back of their Lancia saloon. 'I was driving normally, quite fast but normally, when I came over the brow of a hill and there was a lorry turning broadside across the road in front. I aimed to go around his tail, and got the Lancia heading in the right direction. I got through the gap, but as I swerved back the other way to prevent us hitting some roadside telegraph poles, the tail slid out and just clipped one of those poles,

which sent the car spinning like a top down the middle of the road. Its doors burst open in the impact and I was thrown out one side while Andreina went out the other. The American was left all alone sitting in the backseat, completely unhurt but a little surprised I think.'

Juan banged his elbow while *dona* Andreina was similarly knocked about, though thankfully nothing was broken. The humorous part of all this came when the lorry driver started shouting at the totally innocent hitch-hiker. As he saw him scrambling out of the car alone, he took him for the driver. 'Who do you think you are,' he bawled, 'driving like that! Do you think you're Fangio?'

'No,' gasped the American, 'I'm not, but...' pointing to Juan who was picking himself up off the road to see how Andreina had fared... 'he is!'

Recognising the multiple World Champion, the lorry driver reputedly burst into tears.

That incident meant Juan was unable to drive in the Modena GP, and although he returned in the Maserati for the non-Championship Moroccan GP at Casablanca he could only finish fourth.

But of course, returning to South America with his fifth World Championship title, he then finished the season in his customary style by winning two Brazilian sports car races in a 300S Maserati.

He was 46 years old — and some of us young lions were beginning to wonder if we would ever get the chance to tackle the World Championship without his awesome abilities standing in our way.

September 8, 1957 – Italian GP, Monza. The Curva Parabolica. Juan trying desperately hard to match the speed of the stably understeering Vanwalls of Brooks and Moss in his drifting, oversteering, increasingly outdated 'Lightweight' 250F.

Maserati 250F, Nüburgring 1990.

FANGIO AND SPORTS CAR RACING

I have always believed that during the height of his glittering career in the mid-1950s, Fangio had the measure of me in similar Grand Prix cars. Whatever times I could set, whatever I could make those cars do, Juan could almost certainly go one better. In similar sports-racing cars, however, I came to feel that the boot was probably on the other foot, and I became fairly confident that I could beat him. While in testing or practice his times in a Grand Prix car would often improve on mine, in sports cars my times were usually faster than his.

Neither did he ever manage to win the Mille Miglia, the Targa Florio, or the Tourist Trophy, and so at the time the feeling grew that while Fangio's heart and soul went into Grand Prix racing, he was not as interested – nor as motivated – by the two-seat cars.

Considering that question now, Fangio explains: 'My supposed dislike of sports car racing was largely a whole bunch of coincidences. Look – my whole early background was in Carretera racing which was like running in five Mille Miglia all laid end-to-end. So I was no stranger to endurance driving in that sense. When I raced like that in South America, I never worried about driving at maximum speed, I only worried about what could break . . . so that was a good background for Le Mans or the Mille Miglia itself. When I won the Carrera PanAmericana for Lancia in 1953, I never won a single Stage – yet I made sure I won the race.

'But it is true that I always preferred Formula 1.

That was just a little bit because I liked to sit in the middle of the car. Then you achieve a consistent view to each side from which you can judge placing of the car in corners both to left and right. I would not say it was any significant problem for me, but I always felt more comfortable like that than sitting offset in a sports car, where the perspective one received in left-hand corners was always different from that received in right-hand corners.

'Of course, I would have loved to have to won the Mille Miglia but it was not to be. My destiny was instead to win in Grand Prix cars, and to win more times than any other driver at that time. That was a destiny I was very happy to fulfil; you should not be greedy in life and want even more when it has given you so much.

'But look at the bunch of coincidences which might persuade people I did not like sports car racing. I was leading the Mille Miglia in 1953 until the Alfa Romeo's chassis broke and I was left with only one wheel steering – but I still finished. In 1955, my Mercedes 300SLR was one of the best cars in the field but all the way round it was running on only seven cylinders – yet I still finished. And in 1956, in that badly-prepared Ferrari, I was nearly drowned, and frozen, yet I still finished fourth. In the Targa Florio that year in Sicily, our car lost around ten minutes in the pits with a filler cap jammed shut and the mechanics trying everything to free it – yet we still finished second. If my luck had been with me in all those events would people have said "Fangio does not like sports car racing"? You see, to a large extent it was a series of coincidences.'

142

January 26, 1958 – Buenos Aires 1,000kms. A most embarrassing moment, after Juan had struck oil in Francesco Godia's once-lovely Maserati 300S.

February 2, 1958 – Buenos Aires City GP, Argentina. Fangio's final race win, appropriately upon home soil, was in this two-Heat Formule Libre race. Mike Hawthorn, in his famous cap (left), had won Heat One but his Ferrari's transmission failed in Heat Two. Juan, second in the first part, won the second in his 250F to win overall on aggregate.

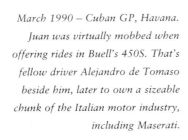

March 1990 – Cuban GP, Havana. Juan was virtually mobbed when offering rides in Buell's 450S. That's fellow driver Alejandro de Tomaso beside him, later to own a sizeable chunk of the Italian motor industry, including Maserati.

1958: The Champion Bows Out

It was a sad irony that Maserati's triumphant 1957 season ended in receivership. The administrators banned further racing, unless a customer could be found to foot the bill.

Meanwhile, Fangio was seriously considering retirement: 'I had first thought about it in earnest at the end of 1955. Mercedes had announced their withdrawal and that would have been a tidy way to end. I was then 44 years old, and I had to discipline myself severely to keep fit, to concentrate, to maintain a decent level of performance – and to keep the new young boys like Moss in their place. Winning was no longer as easy as perhaps it had once been . . . but other factors made me concentrate again and so I had continued to the end of 1957.'

Into the new year, despite confusion about Maserati's future, the existing works cars were entered privately in the Argentine Temporada. Only ten Formula 1 cars arrived, one being Rob Walker's quaint little rear-engined Cooper-Climax for me to drive.

Juan was obviously keen to maintain his magnificent record in those races. During that race he recalls: 'I had taken the lead from Hawthorn's new V6 Ferrari on the ninth lap. I saw Moss coming in that little thing and began driving harder, even faster than in practice, to discourage him. I hoped he would ease off and let me relax and conserve my car, but he kept coming and my tyres began to peel. I changed the rears in the pits but I had not taken my usual precaution of easing off on my previous lap to reduce under-bonnet heat while stopped. So when I rejoined I had lost 500 revs along the straight. Moss had gone ahead and Hawthorn just sat back, convinced he would have to change his tyres. But by skilful driving he preserved them to the end even though they were through to the canvas, and so he won and I could only finish fourth.'

Fangio shared the Spanish privateer 'Paco' Godia's Maserati 300S in the Buenos Aires 1,000kms, but he recalls it with acute embarrassment. 'I was driving calmly behind the two leaders – it was early in the race – and then to take the strain off the engine I took the Ascari curve in fourth gear instead of third. That would have been no problem but at that moment I touched some oil on the track and the car just slid off and smashed in its nose. I did not know what to say to Godia when I brought his once beautiful car back into the pits. He was very good about it but the look in his eyes made me feel I had really let him down.'

In the City GP at the Autodrome on 2 February, in pouring rain, Juan won overall on aggregate time. That proved to be his last race – and, fittingly, his last win – on his native soil.

Maserati's angel paying to keep them racing was an American named Temple Buell. He entered a 450S for Fangio in the Cuban GP at Havana. During practice it darted about all over the straight. When Juan investigated, they remembered it had been shunted and when they measured its wheelbase, one side was five cms shorter.

At that time, Fidel Castro's rebels were on the brink of toppling President Battista. Now they pulled off a great publicity coup by kidnapping Fangio from his hotel, holding him while the race took place, and afterwards releasing him unharmed to the Argentine Ambassador.

As he tells it: 'We got on quite well, considering the circumstances. They said repeatedly they meant me no harm, they just had to make their political point against the Battista régime. Their leader was named Faustino Perez, and after the successful Castro revolution he eventually went into the Ministry of Foreign Trade. At Christmas 1982, when I had surgery for a quintuple heart by-pass, he sent me best wishes from Havana. I think they were grateful I never revealed I had seen any of their faces. The politics were nothing to do with me: I simply saw young people with what they felt was a just cause.'

The story was splashed worldwide: 'The exposure seemed to make me very popular in the USA. In Miami I was given the keys to the city. Then I was given a thousand dollars to go to New York and appear on the Ed Sullivan TV show. It was bigger news in America than any of my World Championships, which I thought was strange.'

A bitter experience followed – Fangio's only attempt at America's classic speedway race, the Indianapolis 500-Miles. Since the FIA, in its wisdom, included Indianapolis in the otherwise all-Formula 1 Drivers' World Championship schedule, there were valuable points to be won there. We had all considered Indy, but decided against it, because left-turn-only Speedway racing was such a specialized art, and there was little chance of obtaining a truly competitive car.

After Juan's second consecutive win at Sebring in March '57, *Life* magazine did a cover story on him. Referring to Indy, he declared that the need to acclimatise to that entirely different kind of racing amongst the demands of a European Grand Prix calendar made it impractical to risk one's reputation, and one's life, there.

Meanwhile, a Monza track race had been organised called 'The Two Worlds Trophy' in which a flock of Indy cars and drivers were intended to meet the cream of the European road racers. But none of our employers – the major Formula 1 teams – saw any sense in building special cars for just that one race, so it became a complete walk-over for the New World.

Then Floyd Clymer, the American publisher of the *Indianapolis 500 Year Book*, issued a challenge, maintaining that we road-racing drivers were afraid of being shown up by the Indy stars. He called Fangio a phoney World Champion for never having attempted Indy, and offered $500 once his entry had been accepted, $1,000 if he qualified on the 33-strong starting grid, $2,500 if he finished better than fifth in an American-made car and $5,000 if he managed it in a foreign-built car.

This all hit the press while Juan was practising for the Reims GP, and his response was typically fresh and honest – 'The money doesn't interest me at all, but if I could get a car similar to those the Americans use I would go there. I just need the right car to race.'

Eventually, Giambertone fixed a deal on Fangio's behalf with a steel company chief and Indy car owner from Dayton, Ohio, named George Walther, to run his Offenhauser-powered Indy roadster in the 1958 '500'.

The trip was a dreadful flop, despite all that Fangio could do to salvage it. He was impressed by neither the team nor the elderly car they offered. He passed the mandatory 'rookie' driving tests with flying colours – as one might expect – but the car was plagued with mechanical problems. 'When I realized the mechanics couldn't get a four-cylinder engine in trim – which is the simplest thing in the world – I knew it was going to be a horrible flop. I also knew that the car was three years old and there was little more speed left in it.'

He impressed all the Indy regulars by trying Lew Welch's notoriously hard-to-handle V8 Novi – Speedway racing's counterpart of the V16 BRM – and lapping quickly on first acquaintance.

But he had spun the Dayton while passing two other cars in one of the four banked right-angle turns. He was

March 1958 – Havana, Cuba. Juan, relieved, happy and discreet, after his release, unharmed.

March 1958 – Cuban GP, Havana. Juan the diplomat as Cuba's soon-to-be-deposed President Fulgencio Battista holds forth, his son looking on between like any admiring schoolboy.

May 1958 – Pre-qualifying trials, Indianapolis Motor Speedway. The five-times World Champion ready to drive under USAC official scrutiny to earn removal of those 'rooky stripes' on his uncompetitive Dayton Offy's tail. This Indy entry became a demeaning flop.

puzzled by the car's behaviour, until he discovered in the pits that his crew had topped up the fuel tank without telling him immediately before that run. Since he had only driven the car lightly loaded until then, all was explained and that was no way to run a racing team. His quickest lap in the Dayton had been 142.8mph on 9 May. Regular driver Mike Magill finally qualified it 31st on the 33-strong grid at 142.276mph, and finished the race 17th.

Since there was in any case a contractual clash between BP and Mobilgas over Juan's obligations versus the Dayton team's, his one serious attempt to race at Indy simply fizzled out. Clymer deposited the $500 due since USAC had accepted his race entry and Juan passed it direct to the Damon Runyan Cancer Foundation.

In Europe, we had all missed Fangio from the early-season Grand Prix races. Maserati had no car avail-

147

July 4, 1958 – Practice for the Grand Prix de l'ACF, Reims-Gueux. Juan's last race. He has just brought in the queasy-handling new 'Piccolo' Maserati after an unsuccessful shot at pole position, a last throttle-blip blows smoke from the exhaust and Guerrino Bertocchi is about to investigate the engine. It will do no good, the car can go no faster.

able for him, and he was entertaining no offers from anyone else – Vanwall included.

The second and last Two Worlds' Trophy race was then run on the Pista de Alta Velocita at Monza on 29 June. Ferrari fielded a couple of special F1-based cars for Luigi Musso and Mike Hawthorn, I had a special V8-engined Maserati sponsored by 'Eldorado' ice cream – which broke its steering at 160mph on the high banking and gave me the fright of my life – and Giambertone had fixed Juan a drive in Al Dean's 'Dean Van Lines Special'. It was another unhappy experience for him.

'I did the best qualifying time and only at the very last moment was it bettered*, and then an American car equalled it but broke a piston. Next morning in the garage I found my car all in bits and one which had broken a

piston rebuilt and ready to run again. My car wasn't ready for the first two Heats and then, in the third, two pistons went after very few laps, so it was another fiasco.

'Everything was persuading me that the time had come. I found myself thinking of Nuvolari as I had seen him in my first races in Europe, just a shadow of the genius I had read about at the height of his brilliance. I'd promised myself I'd never go out like that; when I was no longer able to show my best, I should retire at the top, no hanging on.'

Maserati had a new version of the 250F ready for Juan in the French Grand Prix at Reims on 6 July. 'It was five months since I'd driven a Grand Prix Maserati. It felt wrong. It had Koni dampers instead of the lever arm type I was used to. It had a shorter wheelbase and had lost that beautiful balance of the earlier cars. I was nearly 47 and my leading rivals, like Moss, were almost twenty years younger. Racing no longer gave me the satisfaction it used to, it had begun to feel like an obligation.

* Fangio's time of 55.2 seconds was bettered by Indianapolis driver Bob Veith who was in turn 'bumped' by the heroic works Ferrari driver Luigi Musso.

July 6, 1958 – Grand Prix de l'ACF,
Reims-Gueux. Moment of truth, the
strain tells as Juan has just finished
fourth, it is time to call it a day.
'After 51 Championship GP's, 48 of
which he had started from the front
row, and 24 wins,
it was time to stop.

'In that Piccolo car at Reims I tried hard to qualify on the front row and failed. In the race, I was behind Musso and I saw how he went level with an American driver on the outside of the very fast curve after the pits. He didn't have enough track left and he touched the low barrier at the outside of the curve. As I passed, he went off and I later heard he had overturned and had been killed.'

Juan was disputing second place with me at one stage, behind Hawthorn's powerful Ferrari V6 – which would win – but on lap 24 he tore into his pit. 'The clutch pedal had broken in two at a drilling point and I threw it at Bertocchi's feet. He begged me to continue and I drove on without the clutch. I thought it was letting the public down to see the World Champion driving like a novice; those gearchanges without the clutch were bad.

'I had started my European career there at Reims in 1948, and returned in 1949 intending to stay perhaps one year. I had stayed ten. I had hoped to win one race and I had won five World Championships. My luck had protected me that far: I should not rely on it much longer. I had told my mechanics I would drive four races as long as the car went well – but it was poor. I finished fourth, with Mike Hawthorn closing right up behind me on the last lap as he won. But seeing it was me just in front of him on the road, he held back from overtaking me at the finish line and so let me go across unlapped. I very much appreciated that gesture of respect, from the driver who would, at the end of the season, take my World Championship by one point from the man I had most expected to take my place – Moss, of course.

'I attended the Italian Grand Prix at Monza, and I drove a Maserati 250F again at Modena, but only in private for a BP film crew. My new life had begun.'

Later Life

Immediately after announcing his retirement from racing, Fangio visited Monza for the 1958 Italian Grand Prix. He was greeted as an old friend, an elder statesman, the Emperor of motor racing. He was made honorary starter and I often wonder what must have been going through his mind as he stood there beside the track and watched us on the grid, whooping our engines ready to go.

The entire front row facing him was English, three of us in British Racing Green Vanwalls, the odd man out being Mike Hawthorn in his Ferrari. How times had changed. When Juan had first come to Europe, the scene had been totally dominated by Italian cars and very largely by Italian drivers. Now the British were coming.

Since that time, the wheels have ground on. The period of almost total domination of Grand Prix racing by British drivers, designers, cars and engines has now ebbed away. Today British teams and chassis constructors still provide the backbone of top level motor sport, but, at the time of writing, the last British driver to win the World Championship was James Hunt way back in 1976, and the last time a British-built engine won a Grand Prix was in 1983.

Throughout these three decades of development and change, it's been really good to see so much of Fangio around the World Championship circuits. He has usually made at least one guest appearance, every year, and everywhere he is received as you might expect — but as he never seems to expect himself — as the greatest of all the sport's living champions, effectively as royalty.

It makes no difference whether the venue is the old Buenos Aires Autodrome, Silverstone in England, Monza in Italy, Adelaide in Australia or Fuji in Japan. Wherever Juan makes a guest appearance, his reception is the same — awe in the presence of this living legend.

And yet he has always unfailingly maintained such natural accessibility. While he is always very confident and self-assured, his natural simplicity and warmth have won him universal admiration and friendship.

At home in Argentina, he is known not only as their greatest living sportsman but as a highly successful businessman. He is a major player in the country's motor trade and his acumen, matched by that of his friends and partners, has been clearly demonstrated by the success of his Mercedes-Benz distributorship — established on Bernardo de Irigoyen in Buenos Aires as early as 1951.

Back in those early years, the Mercedes-Benz 170 diesel was a rugged and reliable device ideal for export markets, and with his practical background, Juan fully appreciated what the almost maintenance-free diesels had to offer. Not much in the way of work for his traditional type of 'fix it when it breaks' garage back in Balcarce. Today he recalls those old 170s as being initially 'almost unsaleable, because they were noisy and they stank, but I knew that, once people realized how reliable and economical they were, they would see nothing but the advantages.'

He launched the model on his local market by selling a few at cost to trusted friends. Later, while Juan was away racing in Europe, his company's success back home could be judged by the number of 170 diesel taxis flocking around Buenos Aires — those 'Gasoleros' virtually took over. He was also appointed president of Mercedes-Benz Argentina SA and still holds the position of honorary president.

Mercedes-Benz have always appreciated the enormous promotional asset he represents and they have taken exceptional care of him, which he has repaid many times

Fangio, Buenos Aires 1990.

1982 – Juan leaves the Buenos Aires hospital after extensive heart bypass surgery.

The Fangio residence, Balcarce 1990.

Many personal scrapbooks are donated to Fangio by constant admirers.

over in personal appearances on their behalf worldwide.

But he has never raced again. That's a big difference between us: I was battered out of racing by accident injuries, while Juan made the conscious decision to retire when the rage to race was virtually burned out.

Instead he has concentrated totally upon business and on being the truly retired five-times World Champion. Juan received a great deal from racing, since his retirement he has always been determined to put as much as he could back into it. He has remained keen to foster a future Champion driver, and to help fellow young Argentines in particular to follow in his footsteps.

The first whose career he helped promote was the late Juan Manuel Bordeu, a young man he met by chance one day in a roadside restaurant, where a mutual friend introduced them. The youngster confided in Fangio that his ambition was to race in Europe, and to his astonishment the great man promptly invited him to a meeting in Buenos Aires, to see what could be done.

Bordeu made a brilliant start and was poised to make his Formula 1 debut at Silverstone, when he crashed a Lotus Elite GT car heavily at Goodwood and effectively ended a promising career. I could sympathize.

Argentina endured some difficult times in the early 1960s. The Formula 1 Gran Premio was suspended after Fangio's retirement in 1959, was reintroduced in 1960, but then lapsed throughout the rest of the decade until 1971. Even so, Juan tried his best to maintain close racing links with Europe, and he was very prominently involved with the state oil company – YPF – and with the motor racing magazine *Automundo* in reviving the old Temporada race series during his country's summer – our northern hemisphere winter. He was effectively the draw to attract the best of the European Formula 3 teams to Argentina.

Fangio travelled to Europe in the 1960s to accompany the Formula 3 team sponsored by *Automundo* magazine and his old skills as a mechanic repeatedly helped them out of trouble. For example the warped cylinder head which he showed the new boys how to level by smearing grinding paste over a marble slab, and than lapping it in by sheer relentless muscle-power, rubbing it to-and-fro, round-and-round, until it was flat once more.

In 1975, the Swiss former racing driver Baron Emmanuel de Graffenried organized a great get-together of retired racing drivers and some of the cars in which we had made our names, at Dijon during the so-called Swiss Grand Prix meeting. Juan was star of the show in a Maserati 250F. In 1976 he drove a W196 from the Mercedes-Benz Museum at Long Beach during the United States (West) Grand Prix meeting and he drove the car again at the Nürburgring historic meeting in 1977. That year also saw 'Toulo' de Graffenried organize an enormous Retrospectif jamboree at Montreux in Switzerland, to recall the one motor race run there in 1934. It wasn't much to commemorate, but it was a hugely successful function, and with suitable commercial sponsorship these events became increasingly common and enormously popular with the public.

In his later life, Juan had begun to suffer a mild heart condition, and in December 1970 in Buenos Aires he suffered a nasty heart attack. Once his health had been stabilized, medical advice was simply to take life a little easier, and to operate generally in a more calm and unhurried manner. It's difficult to visualize how somebody as naturally relaxed and cool as Juan could do so. Then, in 1981, while he was in Dubai to demonstrate a Mercedes-Benz 300SLR in the historic Grand Prix meeting there, he

Balcarce 1990 – 'Stromlinienwagen'
in front of the Fangio Museum.

suffered another cardiac episode. Mercedes flew him in a specially chartered medical jet to a specialist cardiac centre in Madrid, where they diagnosed something less than a true heart attack, more a restriction in blood supply. Meanwhile brother Toto had had a successful double by-pass operation performed by an Argentine specialist, Dr Favaloro, back home, and a year after the scare in Dubai, Dr Favaloro performed a successful quintuple heart by-pass operation on Juan. It was really extensive and serious surgery about which he jokes today: 'I went out under the anaesthetic one day and woke up three days later with a new engine.'

All this time, he has remained a proud citizen of his native Balcarce, where he still lives in the house in which he was born, surrounded by his extended family, brother Toto and innumerable nephews and nieces.

The town is certainly proud of its most famous son. In the late 1960s a purpose-built race circuit was opened

Monaco 1990 – World Champions
both, Fangio and Senna.

Monaco 1990 – Fangio and Prince Rainier
in the Grimaldi Palace.

Fangio driving the course, Monaco 1990.

nearby in his honour, the Juan Manuel Fangio Autodrome on the Sierra La Barrosa.

For years after his retirement from racing, Juan also nurtured a desire to make his own small collection of cars important to his career accessible to a wider public. The old Carretera Chevrolet coupés, the special *Negrita* and the great Volpi-Chevrolet Mecanica Nacional car had been gathering dust for years in a corner of his workshops.

Eventually, in October 1979, a Comisión Pro Museo Nacional de Automovilismo was set up in Balcarce to foster the foundation of a Museum in the town. Juan was delighted and touched by the efforts being made to perpetuate his life and his career for future generations. With important exhibits such as a Mercedes-Benz W196 and an Alfa Romeo *Tipo* 159 *Alfetta* loaned by their manufacturers, the Centro Technólogico-Cultural y Museo del Automovilismo Juan Manuel Fangio was inaugurated in Balcarce on 22 November 1986.

Today it stands there as a tribute from both his town and his country to Juan Manuel Fangio, and as a reciprocal gesture of gratitude and affection from the Great Man himself to his townspeople, and to his countrymen.

In his long life, the Boy from Balcarce has travelled far, and he emphatically declares: 'I have had a wonderful and very fortunate life. I regret nothing, and I would change nothing, but I would like to share with others the fulfilment and happiness I have enjoyed.'

I can assure him that here too, as in everything else he has ever tackled, he has succeeded.

Monaco Grand Prix, 1990.

Fangio, in his original bedroom, Balcarce 1990.

Gran Premio Internacional del Norte, 1940.

Plate presented to Fangio by the President of Chile.

Italian decoration.

Decoration presented to Fangio by the Ivory Coast.

Grand Prix of Europe, Nürburgring, Germany 1954.

Medal presented to Fangio by Juan Perón, 1949.

Gran Premio Internacional del Norte, 1940.

Various Italian Decorations.

Grand Prix of Germany Nürburgring, 1956.

Alfa Romeo Tipo 159, 1951.

Racing Record

Date	Event	Car	Position
1938			
27 MAR	Asociación de Fomento de Necochea (3rd in the 2nd qualifying Heat)	Ford V8	7th
13 NOV	400 Kilómetros de Tres Arroyos	Ford V8	8th
1939			
7 MAY	Automóvil Club Argentina filial La Plata Circuito 'El Bosque' (5th in the 2nd qualifying Heat)	Ford V8	8th
19-20 OCT	Gran Premio Argentino de Carretera	Chevrolet TC-Turismo de Carretera	22nd
29 OCT-25 NOV	Gran Premio Extraordinario	Chevrolet TC	5th
19 DEC	Mil Millas Argentinas	Chevrolet TC	13th
1940			
27 SEPT-12 OCT	Gran Premio Internacional del Norte	Chevrolet TC	1st
14 DEC	Mil Millas Argentinas	Chevrolet TC	8th
	Argentine Champion of Carreteras		
1941			
22-29 JUNE	Gran Premio Presidente Getulio Vargas (Brazil)	Chevrolet TC	1st
13 DEC	Mil Millas Argentinas	Chevrolet TC	1st
	Argentine Champion of Carreteras		
1942			
21 JAN-3 FEB	Gran Premio del Sur. Comisión Central de Esquel	Chevrolet TC	10th
2 APR	Circuito Mar y Sierras	Chevrolet TC	1st
1947			
15 FEB	Premio Ciudad de Buenos Aires. Final Mecánica Nacional (Mec. Nac.) (3rd in the Formule Libre Heat)	Ford T-Chevrolet	3rd
1 MAR	Automovil Club Argentina filial Rosario. 'E. Brosutti' heat of the Mec. Nac.	Ford T-Chevrolet	1st
1 MAR	Automovil Club Argentina filial Rosario. Final Internacional Coches Especiales (C. Esp.)	Ford T-Chevrolet	6th
6 APR	Premio Ciudad de Necochea. Final Mec. Nac. (3rd in the 2nd Heat)	Ford T-Chevrolet	Retired
20 APR	Premio Vendimia. Circuito Parque General S. Martín. Mendoza Final Mec. Nac.	Ford T-Chevrolet	3rd
13 JULY	Premio Fraile Muerto. Bell Ville, Córdoba. Final Mec. Nac.	Volpi-Rickenbacker	6th
13 JULY	Premio Ciudad de Bell Ville, Córdoba. Final C. Esp.	Volpi-Rickenbacker	5th
17 AUG	Gran Premio Ciudad de Montevideo. Final C. Esp (1st in the Formule Libre Heat)	Volpi-Chevrolet	1st
17 AUG	Gran Premio Ciudad de Montevideo. Final C. Esp.	Volpi-Chevrolet	Retired
20 SEPT	Gran Premio Primavera. Circuito 'El Torreón', Mar del Plata Mec. Nac. Final	Volpi-Chevrolet	1st
21 SEPT	Gran Premio Primavera. Circuito 'El Torreón', Mar del Plata. Final C. Esp.	Volpi-Chevrolet	5th
29 OCT	Doble Sierra de la Ventana	Chevrolet TC	1st
22-30 NOV	Gran Premio Internacional de Carreteras	Chevrolet TC	6th
21 DEC	Mil Millas Argentinas	Chevrolet TC	Retired
	3rd in the Argentine Championship of the Carreteras		

Date	Event	Car	Position
1948			
17 JAN	Premio Ciudad de Buenos Aires. Circuito de Palermo (4th in one of 2 Heats; results by addition of times)	Maserati 1500cc	Retired
25 JAN	Premio Ciudad de Mar del Plata. Circuito 'El Torreón'	Maserati 1500cc	5th
1 FEB	Premio Ciudad de Rosario. Circuito Parque Independencia	Simca-Gordini 1220cc	8th
14 FEB	Premio Dalmiro Varela Castex. Circuito de Palermo (2nd in the 1st Heat)	Simca-Gordini 1220cc	8th
28-29 FEB	Vuelta de Pringles	Chevrolet TC	1st
21 MAR	Premio Otoño. Circuito de Palermo. Final Mec. Nac. (1st in the Formule Libre Heat)	Volpi-Chevrolet	1st
28 MAR	100 Milias Playas de Necochea. Final C. Esp. (1st in the qualifying Heat of the Formule Libre)	Volpi-Chevrolet	3rd
11 APR	Circuito Mar y Sierras	Chevrolet TC	11th
24-25 APR	Vuelta de Entre Ríos	Chevrolet TC	1st
2 MAY	Premio Ciudad de Mercedes. Final Formule Libre. Rioplatense	Volpi-Chevrolet	1st
18 JULY	2nd Coupe des Petites Cylindrées. Reims, France	Simca-Gordini 1430cc	Retired
18 JULY	Grand Prix de L'Automobile Club de France. Reims	Simca-Gordini 1430cc	Retired
20 OCT	Gran Premio de la América del Sur	Chevrolet TC	Retired
	2nd in the Argentine Championship of the Pistas		
1949			
16 JAN	Mil Millas Argentinas	Chevrolet TC	2nd
29 JAN	Gran Premio Internacional Juan Domingo Perón. Circuito Palermo	Maserati 4CLT/48	4th
6 FEB	Premio Jean-Pierre Wimille. Circuito Palermo. Mec. Nac.	Volpi-Chevrolet	1st
13 FEB	Premio Ciudad de Rosario. Circuito Parque Independencia	Simca-Gordini 1430cc	Retired
27 FEB	Premio Ciudad de Mar del Plata. Circuito 'El Torreón'	Maserati 4CLT/48	1st
20 MAR	Premio Fraile Muerto. Bell Ville, Córdoba. Mec. Nac.	Volpi-Chevrolet	1st
3 APR	Grand Prix of San Remo. Circuit of Ospedaletti, Italy (1st in Heat 1; 1st in Heat 2. Addition of times for Final)	Maserati 4CLT/48	1st
18 APR	Grand Prix of Pau. Circuit Parc Beaumont, France	Maserati 4CLT/48	1st
8 MAY	Gran Prix of Roussillon. Perpignan, France (1st in Heat 1; 2nd in Heat 2. Addition of times for Final)	Maserati 4CLT/48	1st
22 MAY	Grand Prix of Marseille. Circuit Parc Borély, France (2nd in eliminating Heat)	Simca-Gordini 1430cc	1st
2 JUNE	Grand Prix of Rome. Circuito di Caracalla, Italy	Maserati A6GCS	Retired
19 JUNE	Grand Prix of Belgium. Circuit Spa-Francorchamps	Maserati 4CLT/48	Retired
26 JUNE	Monza Autodromo Grand Prix. Italy	Ferrari Tipo 166 F2	1st
10 JULY	Grand Prix of Albi, France	Maserati 4CLT/48	1st
17 JULY	3rd Coupe des Petites Cylindrées. Reims, France	Ferrari Tipo 166 F2	Retired
17 JULY	Grand Prix de L'Automobile Club de France, Reims	Maserati 4CLT/48	Retired
5-27 NOV	Gran Premio de la República de Carreteras	Chevrolet TC	2nd
18 DEC	Premio Juan Domingo Perón. Circuito Palermo	Ferrari Tipo 125	2nd
	2nd in the Argentine Championship for Coches Especiales		
	3rd in the Argentine Championship of the Carreteras		
1950			
8 JAN	Premio María Eva Duarte de Perón. Circuito Palermo	Ferrari Tipo 166C	4th
15 JAN	Premio Ciudad de Mar del Plata. Circuito 'El Torreón'	Ferrari Tipo 166C	Retired
22 JAN	Premio Ciudad de Rosario. Circuito Parque Independencia	Ferrari Tipo 166C	Retired

DATE	EVENT	CAR	POSITION
19 MAR	Grand Prix of Marseille. Circuit Parc Borély, France	Ferrari Tipo 166C	3rd
10 APR	Grand Prix of Pau. Circuit Parc Beaumont, France	Maserati 4CLT/50	1st
16 APR	Grand Prix of San Remo. Circuit of Ospedaletti, Italy	Alfa Romeo Tipo 158	1st
23 APR	Mille Miglia. Italy (Mechanic: Zanardi)	Alfa Romeo 6C/2500 Exp. (Sport)	3rd
7 MAY	Grand Prix of Modena. Italy	Ferrari Tipo 166F2	Retired
13 MAY	Grand Prix of Europe. Silverstone, England	Alfa Romeo Tipo 158	Retired
21 MAY	Grand Prix of Monaco. Monte Carlo	Alfa Romeo Tipo 158	1st
28 MAY	Monza Autodromo Grand Prix. Italy	Ferrari Tipo 166F2	Retired
4 JUNE	Grand Prix of Switzerland. Berne	Alfa Romeo Tipo 158	Retired
11 JUNE	Circuit of the Ramparts. Angoulême. France	Maserati 4CLT/A6GCS	1st
18 JUNE	Grand Prix of Belgium. Circuirt Spa-Francorchamps	Alfa Romeo Tipo 158	1st
24-25 JUNE	Le Mans 24 Hours. France, (Partnered by José Froilán González)	Simca-Gordini 1490cc	Retired
2 JULY	Grand Prix de L'Automobile Club de France. Reims	Alfa Romeo Tipo 158	1st
9 JULY	Grand Prix of Bari. Italy	Alfa Romeo Tipo 158	2nd
16 JULY	Grand Prix of Albi. France (2nd in Heat 1)	Maserati 4CLT/50	Retired
23 JULY	Grand Prix of Holland. Zandvoort	Maserati 4CLT/50	Retired
30 JULY	Grand Prix of the Nations. Geneva	Alfa Romeo Tipo 158	1st
15 AUG	Grand Prix of Pescara. Italy	Alfa Romeo Tipo 158	1st
26 AUG	BRDC International Trophy. Silverstone, England (1st in Heat 2)	Alfa Romeo Tipo 158	2nd
3 SEPT	Grand Prix of Italy. Monza	Alfa Romeo Tipo 158	Retired
12 NOV	Premio Ciudad de Paraná. Circuito Parque Urquiza, Entre Ríos	Ferrari Tipo 166C	1st
18 DEC	Gran Premio Presidente Arturo Alessandri Palma. Chile	Ferrari Tipo 166C	1st
24 DEC	500 Millas Argentinas. Rafaela, Santa Fe. (Mec. Nac.)	Talbot-Lago 4500cc	1st
	2nd in the World Drivers' Championship		
	2nd in the Argentine Championship for Coches Especiales		

1951

DATE	EVENT	CAR	POSITION
18 FEB	Premio Ciudad de Buenos Aires. Circuito Costanera Norte	Mercedes-Benz W163	3rd
24 FEB	Premio Eva Perón. Circuito Costanera Norte	Mercedes-Benz W163	Retired

Date	Event	Car	Position
5 MAY	BRDC International Trophy. Silverstone, England (1st in Heat 1: Final abandoned due to rain)	Alfa Romeo Tipo 159	4th
13 MAY	Monza Autodromo Grand Prix. Italy	Ferrari Tipo 166 F2	Retired
20 MAY	Grand Prix of Paris. Circuit Bois de Boulogne. France	Simca-Gordini 1490cc	Retired
27 MAY	Grand Prix of Switzerland. Berne	Alfa Romeo Tipo 159	1st
17 JUNE	Grand Prix of Belgium. Circuit Spa-Francorchamps	Alfa Romeo Tipo 159	9th
23-24 JUNE	Le Mans 24 Hours. France (Partnered by Louis Rosier)	Talbot-Lago 4500cc (Sport)	Retired
1 JULY	Grand Prix of Europe. Reims, France (Finished in Luigi Fagioli's car)	Alfa Romeo Tipo 159	1st
14 JULY	Grand Prix of Great Britain. Silverstone	Alfa Romeo Tipo 159	2nd
29 JULY	Grand Prix of Germany. Nürburgring	Alfa Romeo Tipo 159	2nd
2 SEPT	Grand Prix of Bari. Italy	Alfa Romeo Tipo 159	1st
16 SEPT	Grand Prix of Italy. Monza	Alfa Romeo Tipo 159	Retired
28 OCT	Grand Prix of Spain. Circuit of Pedralbes. Barcelona	Alfa Romeo Tipo 159	1st
	World Drivers' Champion *2nd in the Argentine Championship for Coches Especiales*		
1952			
13 JAN	Gran Premio Ciudad de São Paulo. Circuito de Interlagos. Brazil	Ferrari Tipo 166C	1st
20 JAN	Gran Premio de Rio de Janeiro. Circuito da Gávea, Brazil	Ferrari Tipo 166C	Retired
3 FEB	Gran Premio Quinta da Boa Vista. Rio de Janeiro. Brazil	Ferrari Tipo 166C	1st
9 MAR	Premio Presidente Perón. Inauguración Autódromo 17 de Octubre	Ferrari Tipo 166C	1st
16 MAR	Premio Eva Perón. Autódromo 17 de Octubre. Buenos Aires	Ferrari Tipo 166C	1st
23 MAR	Circuito de Piriápolis. Uruguay	Ferrari Tipo 166C	1st
30 MAR	Circuito de Piriápolis. Uruguay	Ferrari Tipo 166C	1st
14 APR	Chichester Cup. Goodwood, England	Cooper-Bristol	6th
4 MAY	Mille Miglia, Italy. (Mechanic: Zanardi)	Alfa Romeo 1900 (Touring)	22nd
1 JUNE	Grand Prix of Albi. France	BRM V16 MkI	Retired
7 JUNE	Ulster Trophy. Dundrod. N. Ireland	BRM V16 MkI	Retired
8 JUNE	Monza Autodromo Grand Prix. Italy. (In this race Fangio crashed and was inactive for the rest of the season)	Maserati A6GCM	Retired
	Argentine Champion of Coches Especiales		
1953			
18 JAN	Gran Premio República Argentina. Autódromo de Buenos Aires	Maserati A6GCM	Retired
1 FEB	Gran Premio de la Ciudad de Buenos Aires. Autódromo de Buenos Aires	Maserati A6GCM	Retired
26 APR	Mille Miglia. Italy (Mechanic: Sala)	Alfa Romeo 6C 3.0 (Sport)	2nd
3 MAY	Grand Prix of Bordeaux. France	Gordini 1987cc	3rd

Date	Event	Car	Position
10 MAY	Grand Prix of Naples. Circuit of Posillipo, Italy	Maserati A6GCM	2nd
14 MAY	Targa Florio. Sicily, Italy (Co-driver Sergio Mantovani)	Maserati A6GCM (Sport)	3rd
31 MAY	Grand Prix of Albi, France (1st in Heat 2 for Formula One cars)	BRM V16 MkI	Retired
7 JUNE	Grand Prix of Holland. Zandvoort	Maserati A6GCM	Retired
13-14 JUNE	Le Mans 24 Hours. France (Co-driver Onofre Marimón)	Alfa Romeo 6C 3.0 (Sport)	Retired
21 JUNE	Grand Prix of Belgium. Circuit Spa-Francorchamps (Was finishing in Johnny Claes' car, but crashed on last lap)	Maserati A6GCM	Retired
5 JULY	Grand Prix of France. Reims	Maserati A6GCM	2nd
12 JULY	Vue des Alpes Mountain Climb. Switzerland (Tie for 1st with K. Wharton ERA in first climb. 1st in second climb)	Maserati A6GCM	1st
18 JULY	Formule Libre race. Silverstone, England	BRM V16 MkI	2nd
18 JULY	Grand Prix of Great Britain. Silverstone, England	Maserati A6GCM	2nd
24-25 JULY	24 Hours of Spa-Francorchamps. Belgium (Co-driver Consalvo Sanesi)	Alfa Romeo 6C 3.0 (Sport)	Retired
2 AUG	Grand Prix of Germany, Nürburgring	Maserati A6GCM	2nd
23 AUG	Grand Prix of Switzerland. Berne (Finished in car of Felice Bonetto)	Maserati A6GCM	2nd
30 AUG	1000 kilometres of Nürburgring. Germany (Co-driver Felice Bonetto)	Lancia D24 (Sport)	Retired
6 SEPT	Supercortemaggiore Grand Prix. Merano, Italy	Alfa Romeo 6C 3.0 (Sport)	1st
13 SEPT	Grand Prix of Italy. Monza	Maserati A6GCM	1st
20 SEPT	Grand Prix of Modena. Italy	Maserati A6GCM	1st
26 SEPT	Woodcote Cup. Goodwood, England	BRM V16 MkI	2nd
26 SEPT	Goodwood Trophy. Goodwood, England	BRM V16 MkI	Retired
19 NOV	IV Carrera PanAmericana. Mexico	Lancia D24 (Sport)	1st

1954

Date	Event	Car	Position
17 JAN	Gran Premio República Argentina. Autódromo Buenos Aires	Maserati 250F	1st
31 JAN	Gran Premio Ciudad de Buenos Aires. Autódromo Buenos Aires	Maserati 250F	Retired
7 MAR	12 Hours of Sebring. Florida, USA (Co-driver Eugenio Castellotti)	Lancia D24 (Sport)	Retired
20 JUNE	Grand Prix of Belgium. Circuit Spa-Francorchamps	Maserati 250F	1st
27 JUNE	Supercortemaggiore Grand Prix. Monza, Italy (Co-driver Onofre Marimón)	Maserati 250S (Sport)	Retired
4 JULY	Grand Prix of France. Reims	Mercedes-Benz W196	1st
17 JULY	Grand Prix of Great Britain. Silverstone, England	Mercedes-Benz W196	4th
1 AUG	Grand Prix of Europe. Nürburgring, Germany	Mercedes-Benz W196	1st
22 AUG	Grand Prix of Switzerland. Berne	Mercedes-Benz W196	1st
5 SEPT	Grand Prix of Italy. Monza	Mercedes-Benz W196	1st
11 SEPT	Tourist Trophy. Dundrod, N. Ireland (Co-driver Piero Taruffi)	Lancia D24 (Sport)	4th
19 SEPT	Grand Prix of Berlin. Avus, Germany	Mercedes-Benz W196	2nd

Date	Event	Car	Position
24 OCT	Grand Prix of Spain. Circuit of Pedralbes, Barcelona	Mercedes-Benz W196	3rd
	World Drivers' Champion		
1955			
16 JAN	Gran Premio República Argentina. Autodrómo Buenos Aires	Mercedes-Benz W196	1st
30 JAN	Gran Premio Ciudad de Buenos Aires. Autodrómo (2nd in Heat 1; 2nd in Heat 2. Final by addition of times)	Mercedes-Benz W196 (3-litre engine)	1st
1 MAY	Mille Miglia. Italy (Solo drive)	Mercedes-Benz 300SLR (Sport)	2nd
22 MAY	Grand Prix of Europe. Monte Carlo, Monaco	Mercedes-Benz W196	Retired
29 MAY	Eifelrennen. Nürburgring, Germany	Mercedes-Benz 300SLR (Sport)	1st
5 JUNE	Grand Prix of Belgium. Circuit Spa-Francorchamps	Mercedes-Benz W196	1st
11-12 JUNE	Le Mans 24 Hours. France (Co-driver Stirling Moss)	Mercedes-Benz 300SLR (Sport)	Withdrawn
19 JUNE	Grand Prix of Holland. Zandvoort	Mercedes-Benz W196	1st
16 JULY	Grand Prix of Great Britain. Aintree, England	Mercedes-Benz W196	2nd
7 AUG	Grand Prix of Sweden. Circuit of Kristianstad	Mercedes-Benz 300SLR (Sport)	1st
11 SEPT	Grand Prix of Italy, Monza	Mercedes-Benz W196	1st
17 SEPT	Tourist Trophy. Dundrod, N. Ireland (Co-driver Karl Kling)	Mercedes-Benz 300SLR (Sport)	2nd
16 OCT	Targa Florio. Sicily, Italy (Co-driver Karl Kling)	Mercedes-Benz 300SLR (Sport)	2nd
6 NOV	Grand Prix of Venezuela. Circuito Los Próceres, Caracas	Maserati 300S (Sport)	1st
	World Drivers' Champion		
1956			
22 JAN	Gran Premio República Argentina. Autódromo Buenos Aires (Finished in Luigi Musso's car)	Lancia-Ferrari V8	1st
29 JAN	1000 Kilómetros de la Ciudad de Buenos Aires (Co-driver Eugenio Castellotti)	Ferrari Monza 860 (Sport)	Retired
5 FEB	Gran Premio Ciudad de Buenos Aires. Circuito General San Martín, Mendoza	Lancia-Ferrari V8	1st
25 MAR	12 Hours of Sebring. Florida, USA (Co-driver Eugenio Castellotti)	Ferrari Monza 860 (Sport)	1st
15 APR	Grand Prix of Syracuse. Sicily, Italy	Lancia-Ferrari V8	1st
29 APR	Mille Miglia. Italy	Ferrari 290 MM (Sport)	4th
5 MAY	International Trophy. Silverstone, England	Lancia-Ferrari V8	Retired
13 MAY	Grand Prix of Monaco. Monte Carlo (Finished in Peter Collins' car)	Lancia-Ferrari V8	2nd

DATE	EVENT	CAR	POSITION
27 MAY	1000 kilometres of Nürburgring, Germany (Co-driver Eugenio Castellotti)	Ferrari Monza 860 (Sport)	2nd
3 JUNE	Grand Prix of Belgium. Circuit Spa-Francorchamps	Lancia-Ferrari V8	Retired
24 JUNE	Supercortemaggiore Grand Prix. Monza, Italy (Co-driver Eugenio Castellotti)	Ferrari 500TR (Sport)	3rd
1 JULY	Grand Prix of France. Reims	Lancia-Ferrari V8	4th
14 JULY	Grand Prix of Great Britain. Silverstone, England	Lancia-Ferrari V8	1st
5 AUG	Grand Prix of Germany. Nürburgring	Lancia-Ferrari V8	1st
12 AUG	Grand Prix of Sweden. Circuit of Kristianstad	Ferrari Monza 860 (Sport)	Retired
2 SEPT	Grand Prix of Europe. Monza, Italy (Finished in Peter Collins' car)	Lancia-Ferrari V8	2nd
4 NOV	Grand Prix of Venezuela. Circuito Los Próceres, Caracas	Ferrari Monza 860 (Sport)	2nd
	World Drivers' Champion		

1957

DATE	EVENT	CAR	POSITION
13 JAN	Gran Premio República Argentina. Autódromo Buenos Aires	Maserati 250F	1st
20 JAN	1000 kilómetros de la Ciudad de Buenos Aires (Co-driver Stirling Moss)	Maserati 450S (Sport)	Retired
27 JAN	Gran Premio Ciudad de Buenos Aires. Autódromo (1st in Heat 1; 3rd in Heat 2. Final by addition of times)	Maserati 250F	1st
25 FEB	Grand Prix of Cuba. Circuito El Malecón, Havana	Maserati 300S (Sport)	1st
23 MAR	12 Hours of Sebring. Florida, USA (Co-driver Jean Behra)	Maserati 450S (Sport)	1st
19 MAY	Grand Prix of Monaco. Monte Carlo	Maserati 250F	1st
26 MAY	1000 kilometres of Nürburgring. Germany (Co-driver on 450S Stirling Moss, retired. Joined Schell-Herrmann with 300S, retired. Joined Godia-Gould with 300S when 10th)	Maserati 300S (Sport)	5th
9 JUNE	Grand Prix of Portugal. Circuito Monsanto, Lisbon	Maserati 300S (Sport)	1st
7 JULY	Grand Prix of France. Rouen-les-Essarts	Maserati 250F	1st
14 JULY	Grand Prix of Reims. France	Maserati 250F	Retired
20 JULY	Grand Prix of Europe. Aintree, England	Maserati 250F	Retired
4 AUG	Grand Prix of Germany. Nürburgring	Maserati 250F	1st
18 AUG	Grand Prix of Pescara. Italy	Maserati 250F	2nd
8 SEPT	Grand Prix of Italy. Monza	Maserati 250F	2nd
27 OCT	Grand Prix of Morocco. Casablanca	Maserati 250F	4th
1 DEC	Gran Premio de Interlagos. São Paulo, Brazil (1st in Heat 1; 1st in Heat 2. Final by addition of times)	Maserati 300S (Sport)	1st
8 DEC	Gran Premio Circuito de Boa Vista. Rio de Janeiro, Brazil	Maserati 300S (Sport)	1st
	World Drivers' Champion		

1958

DATE	EVENT	CAR	POSITION
19 JAN	Gran Premio República Argentina. Aútodromo Buenos Aires	Maserati 250F	4th
26 JAN	1000 kilómetros de la Ciudad de Buenos Aires (Co-driver Francisco Godia-Sales)	Maserati 300S (Sport)	Retired
2 FEB	Gran Premio Ciudad de Buenos Aires. Autódromo Buenos Aires	Maserati 250F	1st
29 JUNE	500 Miles of Monza 'Two Worlds Trophy'. Italy (Only started in Heat 3)	Dean Van Lines Spec.	Retired
6 JULY	Grand Prix of France. Reims. *After this race, Juan Manuel Fangio retired from race driving.*	Maserati 250F	4th

Pictures, memorabilia and other illustrative material by kind permission of:–

Alfa Romeo
A.P. Photos
Bernard Cahier
Alexis & Jacques Callier
Centro Tecnológico-Cultural y Museo del Automovilismo Juan
Manuel Fangio, Balcarce
Christie's
Juan Manuel Fangio
Karl King
La Torre, Balcarce, Argentina
LAT Photographic Ltd
Maserati
Mercedes-Benz Argentina
Mercedes-Benz Museum
Museo Dell'Automobile, Turin
Doug Nye
Paul Popper Ltd
Pirelli
Quadrant Picture Library
Sotheby's
Stirling Moss
The National Motor Museum, Beaulieu
Ullstein Bilderdienst

Specially commissioned photographs by Phil Sayer

Designed by Erica Hare and assisted by:–

Louise Jordan
Robert Levison
Gill White
Ghislaine Wilson

Typesetting by ReproSharp Ltd

Pirelli Coordinamento Pneumatici SpA and the Derek Forsyth
Partnership Ltd have made every effort to contact copyright holders of
the photographs reproduced in this book. If they have inadvertently
failed to contact any such copyright holder they would welcome any
information which would enable them to do so.